## BOUNDARY _____

Elizabeth Tregenza grew up on the farm where she now lives near Quirindi in New South Wales. She was educated by correspondence before attending boarding school and university in Sydney. She has worked in education, graphic design, publishing, and now works mainly for Aboriginal organisations, travelling extensively with her partner John Tregenza, who has been active in Aboriginal issues for twenty years. She has one daughter, Kirsty.

Elizabeth Tregenza counts writing the story of Charlie McAdam and his family as a great privilege.

# BOUNDARY LINES

## Charlie McAdam
### and family, as told to Elizabeth Tregenza

McPHEE GRIBBLE PUBLISHERS

McPhee Gribble Publishers
Penguin Books Australia Ltd
487 Maroondah Highway, PO Box 257
Ringwood, Victoria 3134, Australia
Penguin Books Ltd
Harmondsworth, Middlesex, England
Viking Penguin, A Division of Penguin Books USA Inc
375 Hudson Street, New York, New York 10014, USA
Penguin Books Canada Limited
10 Alcorn Avenue, Toronto, Ontario, Canada M4V 3B2
Penguin Books (NZ) Ltd
182-190 Wairau Road, Auckland 10, New Zealand

First published by McPhee Gribble Publishers 1995

1 3 5 7 9 10 8 6 4 2

Produced by McPhee Gribble
487 Maroondah Highway, Ringwood, Victoria 3134, Australia
A division of Penguin Books Australia Ltd

Typeset in 11.5/14pt Berkeley Book by Midland Typesetters, Maryborough, Victoria
Printed in Australia by Australian Print Group

National Library of Australia
Cataloguing-in-Publication data:

McAdam, Charlie.
Boundary lines: a family's story of winning against the odds.

Bibliography.

ISBN 0 86914 355 7

1. McAdam, Charlie. 2. McAdam, Charlie – Family. 3. McAdam family. 4.
Massacres – Western Australia – Kimberley. 5. Frontier and pioneer life – Western
Australia – Kimberley. 6. Kimberley (W.A.) – Biography. 7. Kimberley (W.A.) –
History. I. Tregenza, Elizabeth. II. Title.

994.14

Publication of this title was assisted by the Commonwealth Government through the
Australia Council, its arts funding and advisory body.

Australia Council
for the Arts

*For all the McAdam children, and for all future generations of Australians – Aboriginal and non-Aboriginal.*

# Contents

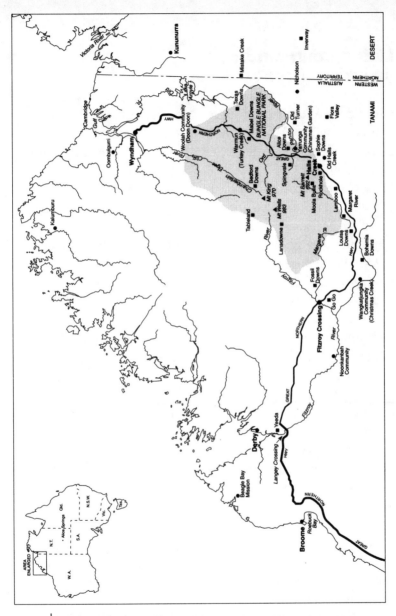

The Kimberley. Shading indicates the general area of Kija country,
but does not attempt to represent specific boundaries.

# List of Contributors
# (in order of appearance)

**Charlie McAdam** son of Jimmy McAdam and Burrel. (Burrel was the wife of Warragunye, brother of Yunguntji)

**Doris Fletcher** Kija Elder; classificatory sister of Charlie McAdam

**Mick Coomb** drover; friend of Jimmy McAdam

**Frank Skeen** stockman; uncle of Evelyn McAdam (wife of Gilbert McAdam Senior)

**Tjulaman** Kija Elder; brother of Mingalkil (mother of Gilbert McAdam Senior)

**Jowji** Kija Elder; brother of Tjulaman and Mingalkil

**Jack Tjugarai** ex-police tracker; brother-in-law of Tjulaman and Jowji

**Jack Johnso**n stockman; friend of Charlie McAdam

**Yunguntji** Kija Elder; uncle of Charlie McAdam; brother of Warragunye

**Frank Byrne** stockman; friend of Charlie McAdam

**Cecil Rose** former head stockman on Moola Bulla Station

**Ernie Sara** friend of Charlie McAdam

**Rudolf Newman** friend of Charlie McAdam

**Father of Roger McGinley** priest of the Pallottine Order, formerly at Beagle Bay Mission

**Valerie McAdam** wife of Charlie McAdam

**Pamela (McAdam) Reilly** daughter of Charlie and Valerie McAdam

**Elizabeth McAdam** daughter of Charlie and Valerie McAdam

**Adrian McAdam** son of Charlie and Valerie McAdam

**Greg McAdam** son of Charlie and Valerie McAdam

**Elliot McAdam** son of Jimmy McAdam and Dorcas Wesley; brother of Charlie McAdam and Gilbert McAdam Senior

**Gilbert McAdam** son of Charlie and Valerie McAdam
**Margaret McAdam** daughter of Charlie and Valerie McAdam
**Michelle McAdam** daughter of Charlie and Valerie McAdam
**Ian McAdam** son of Charlie and Valerie McAdam
**Rusty Peters** artist; lifelong friend of Charlie McAdam
**Rammel Peters** Chairman of Warmun Community; brother
   of Rusty Peters
**Evelyn McAdam** wife of Gilbert McAdam Senior

THE TELEVISION SCREEN was filled by a player soaring above the pack to take a screamer, his outstretched hands pulling the football to his chest a metre above his opponents' heads. He hit the ground a ball of muscle. As the scattered pack looked round for the action he baulked to the left, side-stepped past two opponents, and in a stride delivered a pinpoint pass to a team-mate who was clear forty metres down the field. Straight through the middle of the posts for another goal.

People watching the game on television across the country got to their feet in their living-rooms. The crowd of 80 000 packing the Melbourne Cricket Ground, the home of Australian Rules Football, erupted.

'McAdam!' they roared.

'McAdam!' screamed the commentator. 'McAdam's on fire!' he rasped out, hoarse with his own excitement.

A fleshy supporter of the opposing team gestured in

furious despair. 'Go ter jail and hang yerself, yer black bastard!' Standing near him, a man wearing the colours of the scoring team turned aside, smiling and shaking his head unbelievingly. 'Black magic,' he said, to no one in particular.

In the fiercely competitive game of Australian Rules Football Aboriginal players are well respected for their speed, agility and uncanny ability to read the play. Three McAdam brothers have realised the dream of so many hopefuls to play first-grade football in the Australian Football League. Greg McAdam played for St Kilda, Gilbert played for St Kilda and is now with Brisbane, and Adrian delights the crowds with his powerful goal-kicking wearing the blue and white jumper of North Melbourne.

The MCG is a long way from Alice Springs, where the McAdams grew up. It is even further to the Kimberley, where this story starts. Charlie McAdam – father to Greg, Gilbert and Adrian – grew up in a very different world to his three sons'. His early years were so difficult that he did not speak of them, even to his family, until 1991. Then, at the age of fifty-six, Charlie decided it was time to tell the story that went back so many years before his children were born. This is that story.

# Springvale Childhood

**Charlie McAdam:**    I WAS BORN in the creek on Springvale Station, round about '35 or '36. I never knew the exact date.

When I was born my white father wanted my mother to knock me on the head because he didn't want me. My mother never ever told me that story about the old man – my dad – wanting to kill me. But years later, after my mother died, my sister told me. She told me that four or five hours after I was born my mother, Burrel, and my stepfather, old Warragunye, decided to run away with me. They stayed away from Springvale Station for quite a while, about three months, and when they decided to come back everything was okay. I suppose I'm lucky I'm alive today, because my mother and my stepfather saved me.

My father was the owner of Springvale Station. James William McAdam was one of eleven children from a Scottish family. They were living in Queensland, but he came over to the Territory as a young man. He used to have the mail run from Birdum down to Tennant Creek and back. He drove a bullock team with the mail, and he used to sell stuff too – he was a hawker. He used to sell everything from tea and sugar to rubbing liniment and clothing. They reckon one time he didn't have the right size boots to sell to a customer so he sold him his own boots and went barefoot.

After that he bought the Commercial pub in Katherine, in the days when it still had a dirt floor. Then he bought the Six Mile Hotel, out of Wyndham. He must have made a bit of money because he bought the lease on Springvale Station on 16 November 1931. That lease covered 320 870 acres of country, about fifty miles from Halls Creek. We call that place Balenji, for the turpentine trees that grow there, scrubby little fellers with yellow flowers.

Springvale is Kija country. Katiya [whitefellers] have been there for ninety-six years, but the stories of my people go back to the time the sea covered the land and the Moon was a young man fishing in the Panton River.

When I was a kid, Warragunye, means Left Hand, now, he took me all over that country – him and Yunguntji, his brother – and they taught me these things. As you come into Springvale there's a range of hills, Darrajen they are called, and they run right to Billy Mac Springs. One of those hills is the Fish Dreaming Law. This hill was all under one big water one time. And when the water went down, that's where that big fish, Kundari, the big-nosed feller, got stuck. All the little ones slid down the side of the hill, and perished down the bottom, see. Kundari ngaritj – fish perished.

Just down from that hill on the other side of the road is the creek where Kunjin the new Moon was sitting as a young man, catchin' fish. He was sitting on that stone in the creek with his legs apart waiting for fish to come. And they come straight between his legs and he grabbed them. Aboriginal people still catch fish that way today. Then the Moon took off, right up into the sky.

He was meant to marry a star but he went wrong way. He was in love with his cousin, the black-headed snake. The stars could see him turning his head to look back at the snake on the earth below and they were angry. They sharpened their wallingarry [yam sticks] and they told that Moon if he looks back to the ground again he'll die. The Moon got angry. 'When you mob die you will never get up again. When I die I'll get up as a young man, every time.' And that's what happened. He looked back and he died. You can see him now where he fell to earth on the south-west part of Springvale. He's sittin' there like a big round baldy hill, still lookin' back over his shoulder.

This is Kija Law, but that story goes right through the country up into the Northern Territory. Yunguntji told me to tell these things. He said, 'You've been away a long time but you can still talk the language, Yurudtji.' Yurudtji – that's me.

The katiya called Warragunye Big Paddy, and Yunguntji they called Springvale Paddy. My mother's name was Burrel, but the whitefellers called her Kitty. We are all known as Kija people now, but in the old days Kija was the name for the language and Lungga was the name for the people who spoke Kija. Kija is the language for all that country from Margaret River Homestead, south of Halls Creek, west past Lansdowne Station and back up north-east nearly to Doon Doon, below Kununurra. You can find Kija people all over the Kimberley these days, because they moved them people around so much. My mother was born at Tickalara, near Turkey Creek north of Halls Creek, but she came to Springvale Station as a kid, when Charlie Newman had the lease.

My mother was a tall, good-looking woman. Jimmy McAdam took up with my mother while she was young, even though he had a white wife Clara running the Six Mile pub in Wyndham about a hundred miles away. Aboriginal women had no choice. Katiya used 'em up, for housework, for stock-work, for sex when they felt like it.

I used to live with my mother, my stepfather and all my family at the camp under that big old carbeen tree there, just at the bend in the creek right near the homestead. There was a big mob of us, about three or four families: my grandparents, my mother Burrel, my sister Elsie, my stepfather Warragunye, his brother Yunguntji, aunts and uncles, sisters and brothers. Over a hundred people.

All the kids were born down in that creek, under the paperbark tree. It's still there. In the old days, before blankets, people used to wrap themselves in the bark of the moondah tree to keep warm.

It was no coincidence that the whitefellers built the station homestead right near the Aboriginal camp. It was the best place to camp. My grandparents used to camp up on the little red rocky knob nearby. Back up behind that, up close to the camp, is the flat ground where the people used to go for ceremonies – junba. Old men left a lot of stuff up there for junba – sacred things. The road into Springvale goes straight through the middle of that ground now. Tom Quilty bought Springvale off my father later on. He rerouted that road and he picked up the flat stones off that sacred place to build his garden fence.

Further up the creek right across from the camp is where the big snake Ngamarranye comes out of the ground and goes back in. He goes right through that country. He's lying there, a big smooth rock like a big long slab of cement. Part of him has been tipped on one side. Old people used to hunt fish up the river from there and catch them further up.

The women mainly worked around the homestead, cooking, washing, cleaning and gardening. My mother used to cook in the station kitchen. The men used to do all the other work about the place – cattlework, building yards and fences, all that sort of thing. My stepfather and his brothers were only young men, then, and they were smart men. They could ride horses, break 'em in, shoe 'em, do stockwork, fencing, anything.

I remember I used to have really good times at the station with all my playmates, my cousins and the others. But the best time was every wet season, about November, when the stock work was finished and my stepfather and mother used to take me bush for two or three months. Every year at that time the people used to get rations, bags of flour, sugar, tea, stick of tobacco – for the rest we used to live off the land – and we used to go out bush for about three months. People used to take their clothes off and put their naga on – that's a piece of material cut square and tied at the sides, like a bikini. It'd be hot, and the women would just wear a skirt and be bare top.

Yeah, that was good when I was out bush with my family. There must have been about fifteen, twenty of us – my mother, stepfather, grandmother; old Tommy, my grandfather, who was my mother's stepfather because her father had died; and a few other very close relatives. We used to all go round together.

We used to walk right up to the place called Tableland, above Bedford Downs. That's a long way. If it was too hot, and if it was moonlight, we'd walk at night. That's the only time to walk in summer, on a moonlight night. We used to go right up there, go to ceremonies and – oh, it was the greatest time of my life.

My mother and my grandmother used to show me, my sister and a few other kids all the little things to help us survive when we grew up. We used to live off, well, johnny cake mainly, made of flour from grass seeds. The women walk through the long grass running their hand up a clump of grass and pulling off all the seed heads. They put them into a wooden dish called a lapi. Those seeds are really tiny little fellers but the women keep going until they've got enough. Then they grind them all up between two flat rocks and make flour for johnny cake or damper. Johnny cake is what you cook on top of the coals, and damper you cook under the fire. You dig a hole and put it in. In those days they had no camp ovens; food was cooked on the bare coal or in the hot dirt. It was nice to eat. It wasn't dirty, it was clean – because they used to just hit the ash off after they cooked the kangaroo meat, or fish meat, or johnny cake. My mother used to cook ngawanye, wild potato. We used to eat it fresh, just like a sweet potato. When we were out bush she used to save it up, too, and let it dry, and then she used to crush it to make flour out of it.

We used to really live off the land and it was great. We used to pick the wild flowers off the billen trees and suck the honey from them. We used to get the sugar bag out of the trees, and wild honey out of the split of a rock, or an anthill, and that was beautiful. We used to walk along nibbling the little black berries off the kungka berry bush, really sweet when they're ripe; or sucking on binga, sugar leaf, the white sugar that gathers on some eucalypt leaves. The women used to dig for witchetty grub at the base of the turpentine tree, balenji. On Springvale there was a big melon pad in the horse paddock and you'd always get watermelons there after rain. We didn't go hungry. That country around the Kimberley, you can't go hungry there. There are those big rivers, beautiful rivers with plenty of wildlife. There used to be plenty of wild potatoes, wild fruit, fish, mussels, freshwater turtles, creek goanna, kangaroos, flying fox, and at times there were a few possums there and we'd get them and eat them too. We used to eat snakes too, water snakes mainly. The adults showed us kids how to trap fish by poisoning them with certain kinds of leaves so that they all float to the top. Another thing that we used to eat when I was with my parents out bush was sand frog, just cooked in the hot sand. Have you ever tried frog? Beautiful. Not much of it, but it's nice.

We used to go to waterholes and sit on the sandy banks in the shade of a big old fig tree, or dive in for a good old swim. There were crocodiles there but they were freshwater crocodiles mainly, Johnson River crocodiles, the long-mouthed ones. We used to eat them, because they were harmless fish eaters. I suppose they could harm humans if you cornered them, but my old stepfather used to jump in there and grab one with his hands. He'd see them all there on the bank of the river and they'd run back in, but the water was shallow, maybe four to six foot of water, and so clear that you could see their tracks going into the deep water. He would just dive in and feel around for one, grab him by the nose and tail and carry him out, then knock him on the head with a tomahawk.

My stepfather was really more of a father to me than my white father. He used to make me boomerangs and spears. In those days they used to have mainly two kinds of spears, hunting spears and fighting spears. There was karlumpunye, the hunting spear, and nguni, the fighting spear. The shovel-nosed spear they started making out of steel after the katiya came. Mainly they would use an old worn-out horseshoe for the spear head, flatten it out and sharpen it up. Then there was milinyun, a very, very heavy spear with a combination bamboo and stick handle. The old people used to use that one for cattle spearing. It was so heavy I don't know how they threw it.

My stepfather taught me how to make a spear. First you get wax, black wax out of the sap in nyiyirri, the spinifex bush. You burn the spinifex, mix it up with water, then just keep crushing it and crushing it until it comes to, like a wax. When it dries it's hard as a rock, and you have to put it near the fire to warm it up and make it soft to work with. Plus we used to get these gums off the nyahndah trees [river gums] as big as an apple, sweet and shiny like a toffee apple. When it's soft it's nice eating, and even when it's hard we used to soak it in water. The big thing for them nyahndah gums was that Aboriginal people used to make a glue out of them and mix it with the spinifex wax to really harden it up.

My stepfather taught me how to get kangaroo sinews to tie the spear head on. It's easy. We pulled the sinew from the tail, and we used to chew it in our mouth and wrap it round a long stick so that it flattened out. In an hour's time it's dried up and you just peel off this half-inch wide cord. You get three or four bits out of one sinew. It's very strong, so strong that you can't break it.

One time when we were out bush I went hunting with my stepfather and some others, with a couple of dogs. One poor old dog, her name was Tippany, I think, we used to call her Tippie – anyway she was our goanna dog and Washa was our kangaroo dog. I don't know how many times Washa got ripped by kangaroo claws. If I can remember, my old grandfather was there and a few other relatives. I had my own little spear and woomera.

My stepfather told me, 'You wait here in this gap with these two dogs and I'll go around and chase these kangaroos down off the hills.' They all went up on the hill and I waited at the gap holding the dogs. Half an hour later I could see all these kangaroos coming down. They had to come through the gap where I was to go up the other hill.

I was there with my couple of spears and a woomera. A kangaroo came towards me and I threw this spear at him. Yeah, I got him too, straight through the stomach. Gee. Old Washa, soon as he seen that blood comin' out of the roo, he chased him and killed him. That was one of my proudest moments, because that was my first kangaroo that I speared with a spear.

When my stepfather and the rest of the fellers came down off the hills they said, 'Yeah, you got something?' And I said, 'Yeah, I bin spear him – I speared 'im through the chest and these two dogs bin go and kill 'im.' They couldn't get over how I speared him. They were really happy because I speared this roo and later on we had a good feed.

I'm really, really glad that I used to be able to live out in the bush with my stepfather and mother and my relatives. My grandmother, poor old thing, she used to look after me and she really spoiled me. I was her pride and joy even though I was half-caste, you know. My grandmother and the old grandfather, Tommy, used to always pick me up, take me out bush camping out and all that sort of thing. They had a dingo dog, old Yungu, means devil. I remember him well because he was a savage dog and he wouldn't let anyone near him, only me and my grandfather and grandmother, but he was a good dog and I was safe with him all the time. Every time old Tommy would spear a kangaroo, Yungu would run it down. They used to cook it in the ground. There's a proper way to cook kangaroo. You chuck it on the fire whole and singe all the hair off, then cut the tail off, take the guts out, and cut it up into big pieces. Then you put him in a big hole in the dirt and cover it all up with hot coals and dirt, like an oven in the ground. My grandmother also used to crush up the guts and the tail. She'd have a rock in her hand and she'd crush it all up, and put the crushed up tail and part of the liver with the kangaroo blood into the gut of the kangaroo, and cook it. I suppose you'd call it sausage, and it used to be good too.

I still remember all those things, and when I eventually got married and had kids in Alice Springs I think I was the only blackfeller who had a hole in the backyard for cooking kangaroos. I taught my kids to hunt too – not with spears, but I used to go out and shoot kangaroos and rabbits. I used to teach them how to break the leg of the kangaroo, singe the hair off and cut it the proper way. Greg, Adrian and Gilbert mob can do it today, and they're glad I showed them what to do. They got to like it too. Nothing wrong with kangaroo meat.

There was another thing the old man Warragunye taught me. I had to go through the initiation too. Later on in years, when I went to Moola Bulla, I was initiated, but before that I had to go through the early stages. My stepfather took me down to this waterhole and he said to me, 'You know if you're going to eat turtle I'll have to put you through the initiation.'

He put a hair belt around my waist and took me into the water. Then he dived in, caught two turtles and hung them both sides of my hip, because they had to scratch all around both sides of my hip and that to be initiated, so that I could eat them. I was frightened I tell you. It was a horrible sensation. It only lasted for about five, ten minutes, but when that was over I was glad that I could eat turtle, because the freshwater turtle meat is very good.

It was part of the development of manhood. Even though I was only a baby, that was the beginning of the thing. I had to kill the turtle, and I had to cook it, and I had to feed it to the old people. My stepfather taught me how to cook snake, traditional way, and if I killed a turtle, snake, or whatever, he used to make me cook it, gut it and cut it up. I'd give it to the old people first and I'd eat after. There were a lot of things you weren't allowed to eat when you were a kid. We weren't allowed to eat mussels because we were too young. I couldn't eat them until I went through the second stage of my initiation. It was all part of our life. It was good.

My stepfather used to take me out to ceremonies, junba. He would paint me up, and we used to go and dance. In between the adults' ceremonies they used to have a kids' corroboree, the adults used to sing and all the young boys and girls would dance. But when I went to Beagle Bay, later on, actually I lost it a bit because I left that country.

We used to go on foot to Tableland and all them places, to Elgie Cliffs and Bedford Downs. One time my sister Elsie got tangled up with one bloke there, called Clifton. She was only young and he was young, and when we got back to Springvale she ran away and went back to Bedford Downs with this feller Clifton. I don't know who my sister was actually meant to marry. I never asked her. Clifton was living with our cousin, and Clifton wanted both of them, my sister and her cousin. He was a bit of a pretty boy, I suppose you could say, and he wanted more than his share. Plus they were not of the skin group he was supposed to marry. They were all cousins – well, there's no such thing as cousins, Aboriginal way. They were sisters and brothers. That's why the old people didn't approve. Me and Mum, stepfather, old grandfather, we all went back to Bedford Downs, and ah, I'll never forget that.

The men used to use both hunting and fighting spears for fighting, but the special kind of fighting spear, they used to call it nguni, was long, very fast, a lot faster than the ordinary hunting spear. My stepfather had a big mob of these things in his hand, and a half a dozen boomerangs. When we got to Bedford, there was a fight there between Clifton and my stepfather, with spears. Anyway, I started crying, and I got my little boomerang and spear and I went out there to give my stepfather a hand. My mother come over and took me away saying, 'You can't go in there.' Oh, I was crying for my stepfather.

Anyway, towards the end, that Clifton he had to give in, because the stepfather was a very experienced fighter. Clifton walked up to my stepfather and turned his back to him in submission and the stepfather hit him with the nulla nulla across the back a few times, and then they put their arms around each other and lifted each other up. In our language we call it butel, that means 'wrestle' and also 'apology'. People hug each other and forgive. And that was the end of it. We just took the sister back, back to Springvale. It was a good one, that. I remember when I was trying to fight with my stepfather, with a coupla little spears and a boomerang.

When the wet season was over we would all head back to the station and mustering would start all over again. Us kids used to have good times down in the camp at the homestead. We used to make our own toys, mainly out of tin or bark. We used to cut a bark, or get a four-gallon tin with the top off it, and we used to throw rocks at it, gammon-hit it with a rock, and we used to make our own little truck with tobacco tins and all that sort of thing.

We would go shooting birds with shanghais or bows and arrows, and that's another story – about me and Rusty Peters. This Rusty feller, he and I were born on the same night, in the creek under the paperbark at Springvale. We are what they call jimari, like 'together'. Jimari. Rusty's father was also brother to Yunguntji and Warragunye.

We grew up together and we used to have good times. We used to sneak off with the other kids, riding the goats and drinking goats' milk. One day we had a bow and arrow. I don't know where we got the idea from. We used to get a skinny stick and tie it and bend it into a D shape. We'd break off a bit of canegrass at the joint so it was about two foot long, and sharpen the end of it. Then we used to get this wire, say about three inches long, and sharpen it really sharp on a rock and tie the wire onto the end of the canegrass with kangaroo sinew, and put the spinifex wax on it, like a spear. The spinifex wax and kangaroo sinew made it very strong. Those wire points never moved.

We used to shoot birds or lizards, whatever came our way, not just to kill, but to eat them. Mind you, if we ever got caught with any of these things we used to get flogged. The people in the camp didn't mind us using shanghais but they didn't like us using bows and arrows. We used to fight with them, and we could have got our eyes knocked out or anything. On the white man's side, they didn't like us using any of them. We weren't very popular with bows and arrows or shanghais, especially after what me and Rusty did to that rooster.

One day we were mucking around, shooting things with the bow and arrow. The old man McAdam used to have an old bucket under a leaky tap to give his chooks water. We saw this old rooster there, and I said to Rusty, 'Hey, we'll get this rooster, mate.' We were right near the house. So I took my bow, eh, bang – I shot him right through the head. And this arrow stuck in his head and he went spinning round and round, and out came the old man.

'Come here, you bastards. What have you done to my rooster?' And then he saw the arrow in the rooster's head.

'What did you do that for?' he said. And we said, 'We tried to shoot that tree and that rooster run up close and we shot him.' He said, 'Don't tell me bloody lies.'

Anyway, he didn't flog us but he made us eat that old rooster. We went down to the woodheap, lit a big fire, and we had to pluck it, cook it and eat it. He made us eat the whole lot, excepting the bones, head and all. It tasted terrible.

When I bump into Rusty now, we often talk about that and we have a great old laugh, but it wasn't funny then. We were just lucky not to get a hiding from the old feller.

Jimmy McAdam was in his late forties at that time, but he was fit and wiry. He had red hair in those days but later on it went snow-white. He used to wear an ordinary old blue flannelette shirt and khaki trousers, and an old hat on his head, not curled up or anything, just hanging straight down. He was never one of those flashy types. He was pretty rough in his dress, but always clean – of course they had Aboriginal slaves keeping their clothes washed in those days. He always had a couple of pocketknives and a tin of matches on his belt. In those days you kept matches in a tin on your belt because there was the danger of them igniting with a sharp movement, say a fall from a horse. He kept a tin of Sunlight tobacco in his pocket. Tobacco came in a block in those days. There were two types, the one they used to call nicky-nicky, that was the real strong stuff; the other one was Sunlight tobacco. It was flat, about an inch square, and that's what they used to give you to chew, plus the old feller used to smoke it too. He was always cutting up a stick of tobacco. Sometimes he used to get us to cut it all up, rub it all down fine and stick it in a tin. That's what he used to smoke.

He always wore spurs on a horse and he carried a kangaroo-hide whip with a plaited horsehair cracker. Whips used to be mainly made out of kangaroo, because it was softer than bullock hide. Sometimes the old blokes used to make their own whips out of bullock hide and they were good and strong.

My father used to carry a .38 pistol between the D-shaped rings on either side of the pommel of his saddle, where you put the monkey strap to hang onto. He used to tie the holster there. He carried a .44 rifle on his packhorse and he always used to carry that pistol on his saddle and keep it beside his swag when he was asleep. I remember that, but I don't think he ever used that pistol. I remember he used to take it down the camp but I never saw him actually shooting it. He used the .44 rifle for shooting a killer. When the killer was cut up, they would hang it in the shed and salt it down. There were no freezers in those days.

Doris Fletcher was on Springvale then. She came to Springvale from the next-door station, Moola Bulla. She was the same age as my sister, and she was like my sister. In those days boys had what they call an avoidance relationship with their sisters. I never looked at my sister or spoke to her directly. If I wanted to say something to her I would be sitting some way away from her with my back to her, and I would say 'Nyingan!' ['Hey!'] to get her attention, and speak loud enough so she could hear. She would have her back to me and she would reply loud enough for me to hear. That was how it was then. So I couldn't talk to Doris directly either, but she recorded this story in 1993 about life on Springvale when I was a baby.

**Doris Fletcher:**   I was born on Moola Bulla. That's my country. Jack Bennett, he was a stockman and he went to Moola Bulla, when I was, oh, not quite little . . . He had a contract at Springvale fencing round the boundary. I used to work out bush, round Six Mile and all that. I used to work with Mr Bennett, I was working for him see, I used to be cook.

Mr Bennett went for the Second World War, against Japan, or Germany, I don't know. It was around the 1930s, somewhere around there. When he was called for the war he told me to go to the station and he said, 'I'll leave you here, and you can work for Mr McAdam' – Jimmy McAdam, Charlie's father.

There were a hundred people there on Springvale, I don't know exactly, but there were a lot. There were all working people there at first, and there were no old people. Later the old people come over there. Old people used to camp all over the place on Bedford, all over that station. Then they come back to Springvale.

When I went to Springvale Charlie was a baby. Actually his mother was cook and all that. I used to be babysitter for his mother. She used to cook in the kitchen, for the stockmen and for McAdam.

Jimmy McAdam looked just like Gilbo McAdam, his other son, Charlie's younger brother. Gilbo looks like him. He's got his face and everything. He was a short man, like Gilbo, and a hard-working man, he was. He'd get up in the morning, before the daybreak, about three o'clock in the morning. It'd be dark, you know. Four o'clock we used to finish washing up and all that, and the men used to go out to the stockcamp for mustering.

He was a hard man, this one. Me and Elsie, Charlie's young sister, used to do housework for him. He used to lock us up before the sun set, you know, and wake us every morning early. He used to lock us in the store because he didn't want us to stay outside with the other mob – might get up late, see. *(laughs)* Oh, he was a really strict man, that one. We used to be up at four o'clock in the morning, it was dark and everything. We used to have electric light and all that to do our work. Daybreak the place used to look real bright, and the men used to go out mustering. Those times they used to bring the bullocks in the yard and do the branding.

When the men were away I used to go out with old McAdam on horseback to get a killer. They used to hang it in that butcher's shop under the tank. It had a cement floor and bags hanging down at the sides, and the tank on top used to keep it cool. We built that, me and Elsie now, with one old white bloke, he had one arm shorter. We used to work for him. There were not many whitefellers there, just him and one old head stockman. We used to go down to the creek with two kerosene buckets, just with an arch over here [yoke over the shoulders] and carry water and sand from the creek a hundred yards away, and we put that concrete on the floor. It was hard work. We had strong muscles in those days. *(laughs)* Ah, we're all getting old and fat now.

I was working there for a little while. In December my mum and dad came and picked me up and took me back to Moola Bulla for Christmas. I never go back. They didn't want me to work at Springvale, it was too far. But it was not really too far, you know?

**Charlie:**   The old man used to have a cook at Springvale. He was a one-armed cook, a feller called Bert Dwyer, and us kids used to tease him all the time. He was not a bad old bloke, because he used to give us drinks of cordial and home-made pudding and home-made icecream and all those things. But we used to pinch his tomatoes and watermelons and throw rocks at his house, and sometimes when he'd go to the toilet we'd be throwing rocks at the dunny. He'd tell us to piss off and all that sort of thing but he'd never ever hit us, that old feller.

One day I suppose he got sick of us and he thought, I'll fix these young fellers up. He mixed up a brew, I think it was cod-liver oil or something like that, with a bit of vinegar or epsom salts. He made sure he sweetened it all up and we drank it. Probably about ten or fifteen minutes later we headed down for the creek and we were sick. We were there all day, too frightened to go back and tell our parents. If we told them we might have got a hiding. My mother and Rusty's mother saw what was going on and they came over.

'What happened?'

'Oh, you know, that old Kukuding –' that's what we used to call him, Kukuding, that was old Bert Dwyer – 'he bin give us some sort of a drink and you know it give us runny tummy and we bin vomiting and all that sort of thing.'

Anyway the women went back there and almost killed the poor old feller. We thought we'd get the hiding but it was the opposite way around. They got stuck into this poor old bloke. They were lucky the old man wasn't there, because when that happened the men were away mustering. I think this was about March or April, the time when they started their mustering.

As we got older my father Jimmy McAdam used to take me and Rusty out with him. He had to take both of us because you couldn't separate us. One dry time, about November or December, we went out to Bamboo Spring to pull cattle out of the bog and shoot the ones that were too weak to stand up.

Another morning we went out to the Six Mile Well to check the pumpjack. We had about three or four kids with us – everyone went for the ride. In the evening, when we were on our way back, these lads spotted three blokes killing a bullock. The old feller swung the ute around and pulled up. The men didn't run away, they just stood there.

'What are you blokes doing, killing my bullock?'

The men said, 'We're hungry, Boss, we're hungry for tucker.'

The old man pulled the gun out, and said, 'Righto you fellers, get in front of this bloody truck, otherwise I'll shoot you.'

It was three or four miles back to the station and he made them run, run, run, as far as they could. When they couldn't run, he tied them up to the side of the truck with a hemp rope and almost dragged them back to the station. When we got back he tied them up outside the butcher's shop and flogged them with a greenhide rope. A greenhide rope is a rope that is made out of bullock's hide and it's very, very hard. He flogged them and flogged them and those poor buggers they couldn't do anything because they were tied up. They couldn't run because he threatened them that if they ran away he was going to shoot them.

Next day he got onto the old pedal wireless and got the cops from Halls Creek. The policeman came out the day after with a couple of trackers, Aboriginal police trackers. The policeman chained these Aboriginal men up to a post. They stayed there all night. In the morning they took them off in handcuffs and chains back to Halls Creek or wherever – it might have been halfway, or it could have been back to Halls Creek. But I often wonder whatever happened to those poor Aboriginal blokes. They never ever came back.

I used to often ask my mother, 'Where are them blokes that went to Halls Creek with that policeman?' And she used to say, 'Oh, I don't know my boy, policeman mighta bin shoot 'em halfway or mighta bin take 'em back and shoot 'em in jail, or they mighta bin hang 'em or somethin' like that.' God knows whatever happened in that story.

I remember one night I was sleeping in the camp down the creek at Springvale with my mother and the others when my father came down with a revolver in his hand. My mother jumped up and said, 'Who you lookin' for?'

He said, 'Where's that Arthur?' There was a bloke asleep there, and the old man put the revolver to his head. It wasn't Arthur. Arthur had seen him coming and took off, and that was the last we saw of him. That bloke who was sleeping was very lucky he didn't get shot, because he had that revolver right on his brain box. He jumped up.

'Oh, you Alec,' said my father. ' Where's fuckin' Arthur? I'll shoot the bastard. He's muckin' round with . . .' The old man was messing round himself with the same woman as Arthur, and he wanted to get rid of him. Another feller, MacNamara, killed Arthur, down on the Ord River there, for the same reason.

One year the old man went to Port Hedland and picked up a truck there. Some time after that he bought a stallion from New Zealand. We all went to Wyndham in the truck to pick the horse up, me and a couple of the old blokes – old Smoko, and I think my stepfather was there too. When we got to Wyndham it was at night. Old Smoko said, 'Is there water there?' The road goes over that marsh as you go into Wyndham, they just built it up so the water won't get across, and there's water right alongside the road.

The men said, 'Oh Boss, we want a drink of water, we want a drink of water,' and the old feller, he hit the brakes. Anyway, they jumped out with their quart pots and pannikins and got the water. 'Waagh! This feller water no good.' They'd never seen salt water before, them old fellers from Springvale.

'Hey,' the old man said, 'you want a drink of water, that's the water you drink in Wyndham.'

I don't know how long we stayed there in Wyndham. We picked the horse up and took him over to the Six Mile Hotel. This was when the old man used to own the place, and his wife ran it. He had a bit of a yard there where he kept the horse for a couple of days.

We pulled into the Six Mile, where his white wife was looking after the place. And that's when he caught his wife with another bloke. He flogged that bloke and he busted her up, broke her arm and everything. I saw her next day with the plaster on her arm, and I saw the bloke all busted up. He was a wild ole bloke, that feller, my father.

Another story happened that same time when we went to get that horse. There was a woman working at the Six Mile for the old man's white wife. Her husband was working on the main roads, driving a truck or something, and he used to come in every weekend. Now this woman was having an affair with another man. The old man was one of those blokes that liked to have fun now and again, and this man [who was having the affair] had an old car, probably a T-model Ford, or a Buick. It was late in the evening. They got this blooming car, jacked the four wheels up, and they stuffed spuds in the back of the exhaust pipe. The old man now, he flew into the room they were in.

'Hey,' he said, 'quick, your husband!' This bloke took off out of the room, jumped in his car, *wah wah wah* – he couldn't start it. When he eventually started it the spuds flew out of the back. He put it in gear and nothing happened, it was just spinning the wheels there in one spot. He wasn't very happy when he realised what had happened.

It was at Wyndham on that trip that I saw my first picture show. It was a Tarzan picture show. We all went there: me, Smoko, and my stepfather. The old man shouted us all into the pictures. Halfway through the movie I saw this crocodile thing more or less coming towards us out of the screen, and I screamed and shouted. 'Whoaah!'

'What's the matter?'

'Look, he's comin'!' I really thought the crocodile was going to jump out of the screen.

Anyway, we ended up loading the stallion onto the truck after a few days and we took him back to Springvale, and that was our trip to Wyndham.

I think my father must have changed his attitude towards me when I grew up a bit and was starting to get around. He used to tell me, 'You're going to go to Beagle Bay Mission, you got to go to school.'

Bishop Raible was the bishop of the Kimberley in those days. He used to cruise round to different stations all over the Kimberley in an old bomb car. The roads used to be just rough tracks, but he managed to get around. The bishop probably talked to my father about sending me to this mission. But before they could send me to the mission, Native Welfare took me away, to this place Moola Bulla.

My father told me later, when I met him in Elliott, that when they took me away from Springvale he wanted to take me back and send me to Perth to go to school. I don't know whether it's true or not but that's what he was saying, after I grew up. I found it hard to work my father out.

Mick Coomb was a friend of my father. He came to the Kimberley from the Hunter Valley in New South Wales, droving cattle with John Costello before the Second World War, and he came back after the war finished. His wife Olive was an Aboriginal woman. He still lives in Halls Creek. I asked Mick what he thought of my father.

**Mick Coomb:** Jimmy McAdam used to run the mail from Birdum, just south of Larrimah at the end of the railway line, to Tennant Creek, years ago. He'd come down through Frew's Ponds. That's where Stuart got as far as he could, the explorer. Stuart couldn't find any water, but there's water not far from there in that flat-out country from Dunmarra, and he missed it. He must have been within a hundred yards of this thick clump of lampwood and there's a big permanent rockhole in there. If he'd'a had a blackfeller with him it would have been different. He had to go all the way back to Adelaide and start again, and that's after the blacks hunted him at Attack

Creek. Well, that's the way Jimmy used to come, down through there, down past Crawford's Grave where the overland telegraph feller's buried.

After that, well of course he had the Six Mile at Wyndham. He had a kind heart, Jimmy McAdam. Always had time for bagmen and the down-and-outs. And he liked a joke. I was in the bar one time and two old fellers came in with a sugarbag. O' course there was a bounty on dingoes and hawks at the time. One feller asked for a bottle of beer. Jimmy put the beer on the counter, and the old feller pulled a dingo scalp out of his bag to pay for it. Jimmy didn't bat an eyelid. Reached down behind the counter and pulled out the claws and beak of an eagle to give him his change. Didn't say a word.

Then Jimmy bought Springvale off the Bridge family, Joe and Mabel – that's how Mabel Downs got its name.

You want my opinion? He was a fair dinkum pioneer. Old Jim could take it hard and rough, but he was a man of the time. You've got to go with the time you're in. You can't help it. And that was the day of the hobblechain and the johnny cake and a bit of rib-bone and a kick in the behind and a buckjumping horse. Jimmy survived. Well, he must have had something going for him, because if he'd been that big a mongrel he would have disappeared. As you know yourself, Charlie, anyone that's come into this country and was a bit high and mighty and wanted to walk over everyone – well, next year you wouldn't find him. But Jimmy was a pretty straight shooter and if he promised you something you could bet on it.

No, he was a pretty well respected man, Jimmy McAdam. Course there wasn't many of us to respect anybody. I don't know how the natives took him. Him and one old boy used to walk up and down the fence, one on the outside and one on the inside, swearing at one another. But I think that's why he sold Springvale in the end. It was getting a bit harder to get the work done. Of course money values, you can't compare them now, but it's hard to believe he sold that station for £17 000 to old Tom Quilty.

**Charlie:** That was another thing. When I met my father in Elliott years later he reckoned he was sorry he sold Springvale, because he should have kept it for us. So I don't know whether he changed or what happened. He was all right towards the end. But when he died in 1962, I didn't care. I went to the funeral of course, but I never felt sad that he died. And he was my father.

# Cattle

# and Gold

THE KIMBERLEY IS the remote, vast land that makes up the north-west corner of the Australian continent. The presence of ancient time is in this country, in its weathered ranges and exposed limestone reefs, the sandstone turrets of the Bungle Bungles, and the sweeping expanse of Mitchell-grass plains laid down on the bed of an inland sea.

To the south and east the plains are bound by the Fitzroy and Ord rivers, which channel across the land as a chain of occasional green pools in the dry, and a brown torrent fed by some dozen smaller rivers in the wet. The Fitzroy runs eleven kilometres wide at the Fitzroy Crossing in flood. Beyond the river floodplains the Great Sandy and Tanami deserts roll away for more than a thousand kilometres.

On its northern and western sides the land falls to a coastline of unending sun-washed beaches, giving way at intervals to the grey ooze of mangrove shores. Around these stretches the Indian Ocean – a blinding band of gold light in calm sunshine, whipped into screaming blackness in a cyclone. Its deceptive tides, in parts as high as twelve metres, surge and whirl ferociously around the rocks and islands of the coastal sounds.

In the East Kimberley, thick woolybutt and stringybark near the ranges give way to stands of bloodwood and grey box eucalypts on plains scarred with ridges of red granite rocks and spinifex grass, and peppered with little snappy gum trees. The swollen white trunks of boab trees dot the plains and gather along sometime watercourses. Fig trees hang out of rocky crevices in the walls of gorges.

The country hums to its rhythm of cycles within cycles. In the dry the country seems barely alive, stolid and resigned to survival under the sun, but the monsoonal wet season is anticipated by the sweet flowering of ground herbs, wattles and the black-trunked bauhenia tree. The torrential rains of the wet bring a profusion of flowers, vines and bush fruit. Most plants offer some edible fruit or root, or a sweet leaf to suck.

There is abundant wildlife. Soft-padded red and grey kanga-roos and wallabies share the plains with small bands of emus. The bush turkey, once common throughout Australia, makes for good eating. Overhead the *waak waak* of the black crow punctuates the screeching of white cockatoos. Porcupines, snakes, lizards and goannas move discreetly through the countryside. Rivers and coastline are rich with fish and crus-taceans: saltwater crocodile lurk in tidal waters, the smaller freshwater crocodile in inland rivers.

The country of the Kija people runs through the East Kim-berley, from south of Kununurra to a point above the junction of the Margaret and O'Donnell rivers, near Fossil Downs Station. Springvale Station, where the McAdam story begins, lies in the south-east of Kija country, some seventy kilometres north of Halls Creek.

Customarily, the Kija lived in particular campsites, moving

over the land according to the established cyclical patterns of seasons and ceremonies carried out at certain times and designated places. The oral history of the Kija nation reaches back to creation. Yunguntji, an elder of the Kija people and Charlie McAdam's uncle, has pointed out the shapes of Kundari and the other fish stranded as rocks on top of the Darrajen Hills 'when the big water went down'. Geologists have confirmed that all but the eastern edge of the Kimberley was once covered by a warm tropical sea – 370 million years ago.

Europeans notions of an Aboriginal Dreamtime – when supernatural beings shaped the land – as a separate prehistory overlook the fact that Aboriginal time is interconnected and constant. Things which have manifested in the past are present now and will be manifest in the future. The Law, or what Europeans have called the Dreamtime, is at once the explanation of past events and the structure for a behavioural code on which society is based. The Law, the land and the people meld, so that human consciousness is a part of spiritual existence, and the physical landform is a reflection of the Law, which has always been there. Thus the point from which the Moon left the Earth as a young man is visible in the present, caught in stone in the Panton River on Springvale. At the same time, the Moon is lying as a hill some sixty kilometres to the south-west after his return to Earth, and is also clearly visible traversing the sky on his eternal journey.

The Law has been passed on orally, as part of daily life and through ceremonies. People are bound to specific areas of country through skin groups and descent, which may be reckoned through the mother or father. The family, including all immediate relatives, is the basic unit of a strictly ordered society. Over and above the family, society is divided along strict generational and marriage lines. Breaking the rules has serious, even cosmic, consequences, as the story of the Moon shows. Relationship, age and status govern all interactions between people, a range of behaviour that extends from overt affection to avoidance. Particular relationships, of a brother and sister, man and mother-in-law, man and father-in-law, are avoidance relationships, in which duties like deference, gift giving and protection are understood, but there can be no direct communication between the two individuals.

An individual is addressed by his or her skin name as a mark of respect. When Charlie goes back to Halls Creek he is called Jampiyirn, the skin name for the brown snake. His sister is Nampiyirn, the corresponding female group. Charlie's sons are Jangala and his daughters Nangala. Relationship names – father, mother, brother, sister – extend to all relatives of the same generation, but differ according to male and female points of view.

One effect of this system is that every person stands in a particular relationship to every other Aboriginal person across an area extending from the north-west coast to the central desert, because the skin groups and relationships translate across borders.

Among present generations there has been an increasing incidence of marrying out of prescribed groupings, resulting from the forced movement of large numbers of people out of their country since the turn of the century and from the mobility of the present generation. The invasion of the land by Europeans cut across social as well as geographic boundaries, but the basic structures remain.

The landscape of the Kimberley formed a natural barrier to invasion, so that the nations of the Kimberley were undisturbed by European contact until the 1880s, more than a hundred years after Cook claimed the east coast for the British crown.

In 1879 the surveyor Alexander Forrest made an expedition from the De Grey River on the west coast to the overland telegraph in the Northern Territory. He travelled with an

Aboriginal man, Tommy Windich, whose bush skills and expert marksmanship were critical to the success of the expedition. Forrest called the area the Kimberley, in recognition of the Secretary of State for the Colonies, and released an excited report from Darwin before his return to Perth.

The response to Forrest's report was immediate. Pastoralists and speculators rushed to select land in the new frontier. The cattle drives across the continent began in 1884 with Nat 'Bluey' Buchanan delivering a mob of cattle for the Melbourne firm of Osmond and Panton, from the Flinders River in Queensland to what was to become Ord River Station.

Buchanan was a skilled and sensible bushman who always travelled with an Aboriginal guide (although the guide was sometimes at gunpoint) and who avoided the disasters for which better known explorers became famous. He made several droving trips before he and his family took up properties that included, at one time, Wave Hill, Gordon Downs, Flora Valley, Birrendudu, and Inverway stations. He finally eschewed the settled life to 'poke about looking at land', a red-bearded figure astride a camel and holding a green umbrella over his head as protection from the sun.

Overlanders followed along the Aboriginal tracks that were to become the travelling stock routes of the next century, heading west from the Queensland Gulf country and north through the Northern Territory before cutting across through the Victoria River area. The Duracks, their cousins and associates left Queensland in 1883 in four parties, driving before them 7520 head of cattle, 200 horses and 60 working bullocks. They lost half the cattle en route, to drought and pleuro-pneumonia, but arrived two years later to take the land later known as Argyle Downs, Lissadell, Dunham River and Ivanhoe stations.

Single European landholders occupied tracts of land that had supported large groups of people. The Emanuel family chose the Fitzroy River plains to run sheep, which they shipped to the west coast, and established Go Go, Liveringa and Noonkanbah stations. The families of McDonald and McKensie from the Isle of Skye lost all their stock on a three-year journey of 5600 kilometres from Goulburn in New South Wales to the Margaret River, but claimed the land that became Fossil Downs Station next to the Emanuels in 1886.

Even as the cattle drives were wending their way to the East Kimberley, the government geologist E.T. Hardman reported that his survey of the Ord, Elvir and Panton rivers 'yielded good prospects wherever tested' over an area of nearly 240 kilometres. When Charles Hall and Jack Slattery found 10 ounces of gold 800 kilometres inland, near the border of Kija and Jaru country, the rush was on.

The Kimberley goldfield was proclaimed in May 1886, and by the end of that year there were nearly 2000 men scattered over the area, but mainly concentrated around Old Halls Creek, the site of the original find. The Halls Creek campsite served as the township until it was moved to its present location fifteen kilometres west in 1948. Derby, established in 1883, and the new port at Wyndham, built in 1886 to ship the gold, served as entry points for the miners. But even while the port at Wyndham was under construction, prospectors, disappointed at alluvial finds averaging a pennyweight a day, were selling their horses, wagons and carts for a quarter of their value to enable them to leave the fields.

By 1889 the goldfield population dwindled to 300 or so prospectors. Along with the miners and the pastoralists had come the government officials and the hawkers, doggers, publicans, and other men who stayed on after the gold rush to service the cattle industry. Settlement occurred sporadically, moving inland along the river valleys and plains, and there are people living in the East Kimberley who did not set eyes on a white man until after 1910.

Settlement was accompanied by the massacre of many Aborigines, despite resistance, and the appropriation of nearly all of their land, followed by their gradual incorporation into pastoral operations and other small industries as an unpaid workforce. The settlers made use of the skills and knowledge of Aboriginal people, their tracks and camping grounds, and ran their stock onto grass plains formed during centuries of land management.

As Europeans and their stock intruded further, displacing game and denying access to waterholes and country, small bands of Kija retreated from the plains to the hill country. From here warriors carried out raids on cattle and occasionally on individuals.

The settlers had no understanding of the complex societies they encountered. The two groups viewed the world through different eyes. While the Kija and other nations of the Kimberley embraced the land as the physical presence of the Law, from which they took only as much as they needed for immediate sustenance, the Europeans saw it simply as a resource to be utilised. What may to the Aborigine be the physical manifestation of an ancestor, to be hugged, spoken to and greeted with emotion after absence, appears to be just another rock to a non-Aboriginal person.

A popular story, or contact myth, recounted by Frank Skeen gives this difference as the origin of the conflict. Frank Skeen is Jaru, whose traditional land lies to the east of the present township of Halls Creek. He has worked all his life as a ringer and wears the rolled-brim cowboy hat and elastic-sided boots of the cattle culture. Frank is also the uncle of Evelyn, the wife of Gilbert, Charlie's brother.

**Frank Skeen:**   The cause of it all in the first place was the cattle and the gold. Gold and cattle. They come about the same time. There was an old bloke, katiya, out from Six Mile, digging the gold. He found the lead. Another old bloke [Aboriginal] came along and he saw this bloke digging here and there. He started to cry, because the whitefeller was buggerin' their country up. He went back and got a few men. They speared this bloke down there in the shaft digging gold, and left him there, pulled the spear out and left him.

His mate was cooking dinner [midday meal], leaning back on the tree like this, reading a book. You know how katiya always read a book after dinner? The blackfellers came right around this one. One came front while he was busy reading the book, put a spear right through him and pinned him against that tree.

Then they opened everything up. They found a bag of flour. They didn't know what it was, so they soaked it in the water and used it as white paint. They knew tobacco. They took the tobacco and sugar. They put the sugar in a coolamon, but the flour – that was no good to them, only good for white paint.

●

Not all Aboriginal people went to the hills. In the East Kimberley men and women were taken to act as guides, trackers, station hands and domestic servants. Most taken in this way recognised that resistance other than passivity was useless. Others found their initial fears overcome by the lure of commodities like guns, glass and knives, and their interest in horses.

Aboriginal labour quickly became indispensable. The West Australian colony had requested convict labour well after transportation to other colonies had ceased, but the British Government refused to allow convicts north of the twenty-sixth parallel, due to fears of losing control over them in remote and rugged country. Aboriginal men and women adapted to horse and cattlework with relative ease. Their knowledge of the country, the seasons, the waterholes, and their tracking ability were vital in the establishment of the cattle industry. Working on stations in their own area allowed them to maintain contact with their country, and the cyclical nature of cattlework was not entirely foreign to Aboriginal land management patterns. Cattlework was seasonal in the tropical Kimberley, restricted to the dry months from March to November. During this time stockcamps were satellites of the homestead. From the camps the workers would go out to muster each morning, bringing cattle back into camp for branding and castrating. In the wet months station work was based at the homestead, repairing gear, building yards and other maintenance. The long spell during the wet allowed people to resume their customary lives.

Eventually, the era of life on the stations came to be viewed by many people as a time of wellbeing, compared to the deprivation suffered after the 1970s, but the exploitation and oppression of those years remain part of the living memory of the Kija people.

In the remote Kimberley the newcomers were a law unto themselves, although legislation regulating the treatment and employment of Aboriginal people had been in place in Western Australia since 1873.

In 1900 Aborigines were excluded from the census by the Commonwealth Constitution Act and became officially not citizens. In that year John Forrest, the first Premier of Western Australia, abolished the Aborigines Protection Board set up in 1886 and replaced it with the Aborigines Department, which administered government policy under a series of Chief Protectors.

Under the guise of protection of Aboriginal people, policy from the 1880s aimed to protect the cattle industry, safeguard the labour supply, and prevent the increase of the half-caste population by isolating and regulating Aborigines. The justification for protection was the theory that Aborigines were a dying race. This was first implied in the report of the 1884 Forrest Commission into the conditions of Aborigines at Rottnest Island prison, and fuelled by Daisy Bates's writing in the early twentieth century. It seemed apparent in the sharp population decline caused by massacres, introduced diseases, and a declining birthrate due to deprived living conditions.

Further justification for protection came from the notion that Aboriginal people were inferior to Europeans, unreliable, lazy and unable to handle their own affairs. Each successive piece of legislation relating to Aboriginal people redefined Aboriginality, using words like 'half-caste', 'quadroon', and so on; terms which revealed the legislators' preoccupation with apparent genetic characteristics.

The Aborigines Act of 1905 remained the basic legislation relating to Aboriginal people in Western Australia until after World War II. This Act and subsequent legislation gave far-reaching powers to the Chief Protector and his regional representatives, the local police and Justices of the Peace. They were able to remove Aboriginal people to reserves and keep them there, order Aborigines out of town, and remove camps from town precincts. The Chief Protector controlled any property of Aborigines. Aborigines were forbidden to use or carry guns. The sale of alcohol to Aborigines was prohibited, a restriction which remained in force in the Kimberley until 1971. Police were given the power of summary arrest.

The Act set up a permit system under which employers of 'Aborigines, half-castes under fourteen years, and female half-castes' were required to hold a permit for employment, or hold a permit and enter into an agreement with the Aboriginal employee. Agreements were not compulsory for employment of women or youths under eighteen years. No provision was made for workers' wages, food or accommodation, although by 1936 the Act required employers to contribute to a medical fund, provide free transport for medical treatment, and maintain a first-aid kit.

The reality for the Aboriginal people of the Kimberley was that the laws, of which they knew nothing in any case, were administered by local police and Justices of the Peace, who were unlikely to prosecute Europeans and were frequently involved themselves in abuses of Aboriginal people.

The pastoralists saw the bands of people who did not 'sit down' (stay) on the stations as an ongoing threat, particularly for cattle spearing, and they made repeated requests to the West Australian government to contain the problem. The official police response to cattle spearing – arresting whole groups, putting the men in neck chains and marching them to the nearest magistrate or Justice of the Peace for summary sentencing – had little effect. The unofficial response of pastoralists and police was indiscriminate slaughter of groups of people.

In 1910, after repeated submissions from the pastoralists, the West Australian government resumed twenty-eight pastoral leases comprising over a million acres near the Wyndham–Halls Creek road, and established a ration station with the expressed intentions of deterring cattle killing on neighbouring stations and 'civilising' the local Aborigines.

The station was given the name Moola Bulla, meaning 'plenty tucker' according to Daisy Bates. Its dominant feature is the mountain the Kija call Ngarrawarnji. There was already an Aboriginal population on Moola Bulla, and from 1910 to 1920 numbers of Kija people from the surrounding area were brought into the station.

Besides training people for semi-skilled employment, Moola Bulla served to isolate children of mixed descent from their Aboriginal families, supposedly to assist their transition into European society. Numbers of 'half-caste' children, and women, were removed there. Moola Bulla was also used as a detention centre for men from all over the Kimberley convicted of a variety of offences. This incongruous population of different cultures meant that some people left the station again soon after they were brought in.

Among the Kija people moved to Moola Bulla were the families of Yunguntji and his sister, and of Tjulaman and Jowji, whose younger sister Mingalkil would later become the mother of Gilbert McAdam, Charlie's younger brother. Although they had heard about the katiya, it was on Moola Bulla that Yunguntji, Tjulaman and Jowji first saw a white man, perhaps forty years after the first Europeans arrived in the Kimberley.

Yunguntji was taken away from Moola Bulla by a dogger called Barney O'Leary not long afterwards. He estimated he was about ten at the time. Jowji did not stay long at Moola Bulla; he ran away with a group of other people. Tjulaman stayed, and worked most of his life as a ringer there.

Now elderly men, Tjulaman and Jowji live in a camp on the outskirts of Halls Creek. Tjulaman is tall, spare-framed, dressed in the pastoralist's uniform of tweed jacket and broad-brimmed hat, but his feet are bare. His dwelling, like his clothes, comprises cast-offs, wire mesh, bags and planks of wood. He speaks with an old-fashioned courtesy that does not quite belie Charlie's *sotto voce* comment that he is a man to be reckoned with, who in his youth speared a man to death. Jowji, his younger brother, is rounder, irascible, but Tjulaman does most of the talking.

He recalls a feeling of panic among the people when the katiya were moving into Kija country. As children, the brothers moved with their family from one range of hills to the next, avoiding the white men.

**Tjulaman and Jowji:**   Now we will sing you a song of this country, 'bout the rivers and mountains. We sing you that corroboree belonga our side. [The men chant the song of the origin of their country, beating time with clapsticks.]*

*In this song the old men were calling the country, naming one place after another, each name acting like a mantra. The meaning of the song is lost in

**Tjulaman:** That's the Kija Law we tell you. Do you understand that? You put it in that book. And you put in that book that Tjulaman and Jowji sang this song. Not our katiya names, not Tiger and Pilot, they rubbish names. I Tjulaman, and my brother, Jowji.

My friend, I will tell you this story. People said we were wild. We *were* wild. I know. I went wild myself.

We were moved from our own country. The country of the Kija goes right across, right up Ord River, across nearly to Wyndham and back down – all the Chamberlain River country, all over Tableland, Turkey Creek, Bedford Downs, Lansdowne, Moola Bulla, Springvale. All same thing, Kija country.

I was born on Lansdowne Station, that hill over there, I don't know the white man's name. River come there (*drawing on map on ground*), another river goes this way. It flows into Fitzroy Crossing.

Going back, when my grandfather and grandmother were alive, there were hundreds of us. I was a kid then, might have been five, just a little kid. We had no [white man's] food. We used to get a coolamon full of panari [bush potato], and we'd get honey from the ground and honey from trees. There was a lot of food over there – goanna, turkey, fish too. We didn't know tea and sugar, milk, biscuit, nothing at all. Just all like that.

When the katiya came over here from Queensland he took the place over, whatever place he wanted. There were a lot of natives here, close to thousands there were. We went to the big hills over there, frightened of white man. They were taking natives, trying to close them in on the station or something like that. We didn't see them. We heard from the old men something was wrong. They had an idea.

English translation. It is a statement of belonging to the northern part of the Kija land shown in the map at the front of this book.

They were chasing blackfellers all the time, all over the place, all the whitefellers. People went wild after that. Wild! They went crazy, frightened of the white man.

We ran into the caves – those fish hills there. The caves were a warm place. Under the rocks they call Lansdowne there's one that's got a good cave inside – a lot of room inside, it goes deep, a long way back, [and we used to] sleep inside in the rain time. We had turkey, goanna, porcupine, beef – all there, all cooking inside the cave.

Then I was taken by the government. The government took people and put them in Moola Bulla. It was the government that took them, from right up to Wyndham and right back there, put them in Moola Bulla, even pensioners too. We got no money, but hard work, that's all.

●

In the end, Tjulaman said, it was people who spoke Kija who came out to encourage them to go to the station. Official use of Aboriginal people as trackers and to communicate with local people was common practice. The Native Police played a crucial role in quelling Kimberley resistance in the police raids in the 1890s. The resistance fighters Pigeon (Sandamarra) and Major were both tracked and shot by Aborigines. Because black troopers had the same bushcraft skills as the people they pursued, they came to be feared by other Aboriginal people far more than the ordinary police force.

As with the Aborigines who worked on the stations, there was a variety of reasons for working with the police, not least being the fact that it represented a chance for survival. Once enlisted, there was no way out of the Native Police. Discipline was brutally enforced, deserters were shot.

Aborigines continued to be used as an adjunct to the police force in the Kimberley well after the last Native Police contingent in the east, on Cape York Peninsula, was disbanded just before World War I. In the Native Police it was policy to take men away from their own country and mix different language groups, to capitalise on inter-tribal fears and prejudices and to prevent collusion against white officers.

Jack Tjugarai is a Gurindji man. Gurindji land is some 300 kilometres to the east of Halls Creek, in the Victoria River area. Jack's father and grandfather were taken to Halls Creek to work as trackers, and Jack simply followed in their footsteps. He married a Kija woman, the sister of Tjulaman and Jowji, and lives in a camp at Halls Creek. His bearing is military still. His work with the police consisted mainly of tracking and helping to catch petty criminals. These days, when he tells his story, there is conflict between his pride in a job that he did well and the shame he felt when he witnessed the police treatment of young men he had helped to catch.

**Jack Tjugarai:** It happened to us too. They bin chase 'em up, in our country, chasing blackfellers – take little kids, bring them into the government station and keep them. My father worked for police. We used to live in old Halls Creek. Them policemen make it hard for people. Kija people, they used to come into the Moola Bulla settlement and do their time – two year, like prison. I seen that place. They came from Ord River, Nicholson, other place out here, 'nother station. They used to come to Moola Bulla. They rounded them up, they tell 'em people got to go there now.

Blackfeller they used to string them like to that tree over there, sometime policeman give 'em a good hiding. All together, one line, long chain. Government lookin' for them, they get 'em and line 'em up, put 'em in a chain, tie two together. Get a bag of cement, hard one, 'bout that big. And they were heavy. Tie it round their shoulders.

•

The sense of natural justice is a strong underlying principle of Aboriginal Law. Humour, the counter-punch of adversity, is never far away in Aboriginal discussions of the peculiarities of British justice.

**Tjulaman:** Say a blackfeller kills someone. Ring up the policeman, he'll be there.

'Where's the murderer? Right.' He takes the murderer over in the trees and gives 'im a good hiding, then he takes 'im to Moola Bulla.

**Jack Tjugarai:** Whitefellers that are murderers, policeman ties 'im up and puts 'im on the two-engine plane to Darwin. It's still the same today.

●

The katiya process, the men say, is full of contradictions. In comparison, Kija justice and its system of payback is more straightforward and leaves everything square. The Kija maintained customary Law and ceremonial life on Moola Bulla, despite the prevailing view that the culture was dying out along with its people. In fact there was a period of adaptation to the invading culture, on the missions, reserves and stations. The people took on board the demands placed on them by Europeans and picked up their normal lives when possible. Ceremonies continued at night and on weekends, especially on Moola Bulla. Doris Fletcher, who lived on Moola Bulla until 1955, commented, 'There was always something going on there – every night. I miss that the most, now.'

**Tjulaman:** A blackfeller can't get away from his Law. One young feller at Moola Bulla killed a girl. It was race time. All the katiya go into horseraces at Halls Creek once a year. Some blackfellers go too. They bring that girl into hospital and she

died there. All the relations, you know how we go out somewhere and talk:

'Who you reckon murderer?'

'Only one feller, that feller from Broome.'

'We take him out bush, hunting.'

Old Sloper, he said, 'I'll go in the front, waiting there . . .'

They go out hunting but they didn't find a kangaroo. They
coming back now, and they could see that old man Sloper
behind the rocks, but they keep this boy busy talking to him.
They come closer to the rocks. They go past that rock. Old
Sloper, he's got his spear hooked now. One feller looked
back, 'Give him room, give him room . . .'

He got him right through the back, the spear went right
through and that steel [shovel-nose spear], it bent inside. He
couldn't walk.

George the manager, he found him and got a car and
picked him up, and they couldn't pull that spear out of his back.
They sent him to the big hospital and when they pulled that
thing out of him, he died.

Another feller, they bin take him out bush, they bin get a pick-
handle and hit him right across the head – finish. They put 'im
right across the road and leave him there. Police reckon by
accident – car run over 'im.

**Charlie:** But you know what they did that for – he bin
showing the katiya all the things, sacred places, that's why
they kill him. He was selling minerals to all the whitefellers, this
mineral exploration mob. That's why they got rid of him.
They chucked his body on the road after they killed him. The
bloke that killed him, they got him too. It was a payback.

**Tjulaman:** That's right, all square, finished.

**Jack Tjugarai:** When they do it blackfeller way, you can't see how it's done. They take his dirty clothes, put a bit of bloodstain on them, and put 'em in a hole. Then burn 'em. Might be three or two weeks, that man get very sick, die, and finish. Everybody square.

And another style, my mob [Gurindji]. They get your clothes and take them to the waterhole. There's a snake in there. They dig in the right place and give the snake your clothes, and later on the cloud starts. You see him rolling along, coming along, and they say, 'He's coming now, that snake,' and that man finish there. You see that man, he's sick and he die.

●

Retaliation to cattle spearing does not explain the indiscriminate killing of large groups of people that went on into this century. The last recorded massacre of Aboriginal people was by police in the Pilbara in 1928, but the Kija recall twelve mass killings in their country, at least two of which occurred in the 1930s, according to the people of Halls Creek. At one site on the banks of the Panton River, near Chinaman Garden, the place of massacre is still clearly visible. The eastern bank grows thick with Flinders grass, except for a circular patch about ten metres in diameter where the vegetation changes to scrubby bush and grasses common to areas of regrowth after soil degradation. In this case the degradation was by fire, the burning of the bodies of a camp of Kija people who were surrounded by horsemen and shot there. The soil itself at the base of the plants is charred and fine, like black silt. Thousands of small fragments of bone are scattered over the area. Across the river from the site there is a rough climb up the steep slope of a hill, through spinifex grass and boulders, to the mouth of a substantial cave three metres high by seven metres wide. The cave extends back into a maze of crevices and tunnels. The roof is still blackened by fire.

**Charlie:**   One old feller got away. Must have been coming back from hunting and saw them or something. He ran right across the creek bed and up the hill through those rocks and spinifex into a cave. They chased him up there, fired a few shots into the cave, then they built a big heap of wood in front of the cave and set fire to it to smoke him out. But he got away when it got dark. He got cold stones so he could step on them to get out. He went up to Springvale then.

The people heard about what had happened. That night they were wailing, mourning for the dead. Then this old feller walks into the camp, and that's when they really started wailing because they thought he was a ghost. He lived for a long time in Turkey Creek after that. They used to call him Manangin. Means 'fire man'.

•

Like Frank Skeen, Jack Johnson is a Jaru man who has worked all his life with cattle and has a reputation for horse-manship.

**Jack Johnson:**   That place [on the Panton River] where they burnt the people, you can see it now. For a long time it was just bare dirt. The grass would not grow for all the grease, human fat, that was burnt there. It was just like the killing yards, when they burn the head and guts and everything. I met that old Fire Man, Manangin, a few years back when I was in the stock-camp, working as a ringer on Alice Downs. He was the only one that got away.

If the people killed one beast in those days then they had to get a hundred blackfellers. They had to destroy them. There were a lot of our people in those days, a big mob.

Before that Panton River massacre, some of them were shot down there in our country near Keith River. The old people reckon there were a lot of them hanging up in the tree. They tried to climb up the tree to get away – bang. Dead and gone. They shot them and just left them there hanging in the tree.

At Hangmans Creek, down the back of Lamboo Station, they got over a hundred men and women and children. You can still see the marks of the chain on that big tree – carbeen tree. Somebody speared some cattle and they went out to the camp and rounded them up. They didn't know what for, poor buggers didn't know what the katiya were going to do to them. The boss got a pit dug down there, about fifteen to sixteen feet. Aboriginal people had to go in there and katiya shot them until they couldn't shoot any more. They got horses and donkey chains and they pulled them up over the tree until the water comes out of them and they're dead. Then they drag them over there and chuck them in the pit. They put 'em down there, got a drayful wood, and they burned those poor buggers down there.

They got easy hundred, properly. They [old people] was talkin' about a lot of people that was killed there with the same mob. They killed everything they had. They didn't burn the dogs. They leave all the dogs for scalps.

Some wouldn't get in that pit there, some of them sit up on top there, but they shot them, put wood over them, kerosene, and burn them.

I went out to Hangmans Creek with my wife in 1983 and you could still see the tree where they hung the Aboriginal people with the donkey chains. Limb got dried up. Ringbarked by chains from hanging people up.

**Frank Skeen:**   None of them could speak English, and they couldn't understand what the katiya said. They got rid of the lot, blew the lot up, one time – over and done with.

**Jack Johnson:**   That might be the right rule for them. It's not Aboriginal way of doing things. Aborigines believe something else. This [story is about] my grandmother and grandfather, my mother's father. My mother was born up the river a bit near the Ord River junction.

They told me about my grandfather and my granny, my mother's father and mother, shot, just because someone speared some cattle. When they brought the cattle down there to the water, these fellers thought, Oh, beef – come on we'll get one. Bang, with their spear. When the katiya found the few cattle they speared, that mob just went back and got the rest of them, got their rifles and blew them up while they were camping around the campfire. They didn't know what happened.

Lucky my mother didn't get shot. She was just a baby. After that another grandfather, an old man, went back to see if his brother was alive or not, but every one of them there was shot. Just one kid was alive, only a baby, my grandmother's kid, the rest of them dead.

He picked her up and took her back out in the hills, back to Turner Station, not far. Old Bert Lawford was manager of Turner and he was a bad one too, Bert Lawford. But in those days they were all bad – you couldn't trust anybody.

They reckon it's our turn to be good friends, but there's something wrong, eh?

●

Charlie McAdam's uncle, the brother of Yunguntji and Warragunye, was one of a group of men killed on Bedford Downs somewhere between 1930 and 1938. This massacre is still widely discussed in the East Kimberley and is the most recent in living memory. Yunguntji says that he was a teenager working on Bedford Downs when it happened.

Now a frail, bony little man with snow-white hair whose appearance belies his stature in the community, Yunguntji lives in Chinaman Garden (Yarrunga Aboriginal Community) with his wife and family. He has seen it all, from the invasion of

his country by the pastoralists to the miners digging diamonds out of creek beds at Argyle to the north. Yunguntji
walks with difficulty these days, leaning on his stick, but
there is a spark in his old eyes and authority in his tone.

**Yunguntji:** Whitefellers are all right. Lot of mad people
early days, you know. All them Queenslanders were a hard
mob. They came down that main road from Wyndham
shootin' blackfellers, first one side and then the other. They've
settled down a bit now. We all same, really, white and Aborigine.

I was born Old Bedford – that's Kija country too. Same
thing. I bin grown with the white man, you know. He bin
grow me up, one old katiya called Barney O'Leary. I used to call
him Father. My father and mother was at Moola Bulla. We all
lived together there, and then that katiya come and split us up.
I was a little kid. Barney O'Leary come down the creek an' he
said, 'I think I'll take this kid.' Nothing you could do. He took
me to Lansdowne. I met him when he's just a dogger, killing
dogs. Following the dogs around. That's how we lived, with the
dog scalps, catching tucker and things, you know. No money, no
anything. Well, he bin getting the money off the dogs, I don't
know how much. We didn't know. A pound, something like that,
but [he] didn't give us any. Just got enough to keep us in
tucker. He used to sell them get some money. He used to go
himself to get them rations.

Later on he come back to Moola Bulla and got my sister. My old
sister, he was livin' with her. And one old blind woman, we had to
pull 'im around everywhere. [S]he bin passed away now.

We bin go all over this country all around the place. We
bin make a place over there. Big mud house in the side of the hill
– pick up all the iron beds and make a homestead. It's still standing there now.

When my old father, I used to call him Father, old Barney
O'Leary, got horn here [through his knee], straight through, he

gone somewhere. I don't know where he went – he went away and left me, you see. Paddy Quilty come and picked me up and take me to Bedford [where the massacres occurred].

I bin come here, to Bedford Downs [as a] kid, you know, and I bin grow up here. Grow up here, ride the horse and things right here.

This whole story started here, at that gate. They chained them up there, that old Quilty, old Paddy, and all his mob, that Tableland mob.

They might be here now. I woke up last night, there was one blue light in the fire. I might be muddled, might be the fire I s'pose, but they was showing blue, you know? Only one blue light. I didn't take much notice.*

When they killed the old bullock – not bullock, milker – in Bedford there, they bin sent to jail for that, to Wyndham, and come straight back again. Put a licence on 'em, that licence here, 'round their neck. Not really a licence but a . . . ticket.

I had a look at my big brother. 'Hey, what's this you got?'

'Oh, don't touch it.'

And I told him, you know, I said, 'This is rubbish! Dog one!' And he said, 'Nah, leave it, that's mine!'

All right. Leave it alone. I didn't say nothing. Otherwise he might bin want to give you a hiding. He talk big way, see. Like a kid talk.

They all had that ticket. I told them, 'Ah, that's only rubbish.' I had a fair idea. Oh, I was a good size feller, big [enough] to ride a horse. I was riding a horse around then, you know, going around with the horses. I tried to tell my brother but he bin get wild and said, 'Ah, that's my thing, leave it there.' And he find himself in the fire.

*This account was given on Bedford Downs, not far from the site of the massacre. Yunguntji explains that the blue light may have been the appearance of one of the spirits of those who were killed there.

That morning they grab an axe, sharpen it up, then they – ah, they only tell them they were going to get some wood. But you know what happened. You know that place where they bin, you know, make a big fire.

They didn't let me come. I wanted to, on that dray, and one katiya bloke, old Barney O'Leary, told me, 'No, don't come. We got to cart too many wood.' I was a lucky man.

And that gate we come to, with that Bedford homestead one side? They come there. That white bloke bin come there, with a mule – Paddy Quilty – and he tell 'em whole lot get off, and put the chain around their neck, and he bin pull a gun out. Yeah, he bin put a chain around them, chained the lot, at that gate there. This other mob bin come from over here, Tableland – that mob of katiya bin come. Scotty Sadler, boss on Tableland Station. Another katiya – Salmond. Another feller, katiya, I can't remember his name. The night before they camped on top, hilltop there [Mt King], and meet up here.

They tell 'em they going to get wood. Make a fire there, dinner camp. That was the place they had dinner, those two snappy gum trees. We call them dalngarrlye tree, in Aboriginal way. I know those trees, near the road, not far off the road. They poisoned the lot there, all of them. That's the place they bin poison them. (pause)

They bin poison them, made a big stew for them. They put strychnine in that stew. Ah, they bin staggering everywhere, fall over with the chain, and they bin start shooting them, you know? Staggerin' everywhere, fall over and all. Other mob shoot them. Yeah. That's what they done.

I think they put them all in the dray, all the poisoned mob, and they cart 'em all away with the dray, away over there. (pause)

One old bloke, he died now anyway, he's the feller bin come down and have a look, you know – the first one. Poor old feller been there. Called Doctor. [This was Yunguntji's father, a man of high degree.] *(pause)* Old man. He went up, he seen the smoke, he went up and looked. And he went back, and tell them people, all the bad luck, you know? 'They're all burned.' He's the only one find this mob. And he go back and tell them, other mob, that night.

We bin all go to sleep. They bin leave me with the bag, covered me up with the bag. All the people ran off, right from the homestead. All bin get away and leave me. They wouldn't kill me, Paddy Quilty and all them mob. He's the one, now, dangerous bugger, Paddy Quilty.

I was riding with a horse and see the fire place there. Had no grass, you know. You can't see it now. The big rain came here and grow everything up, and take the thing away, you know? Wiped the country over. You can hardly know where the place is, now.

I bin live with them cheeky katiya now. That Paddy Quilty now. They bin know me very well too.

Then I had to go to Springvale and live there – really grew up there. I was riding a horse, them days, mustering and riding, breaking horse in and all that.

Old Joe Bridge was there. Oh there was a big mob there – all the Bridge mob. He had a lot of kids – Norman Bridge, Charlie Bridge, and Katie Bridge, and Mabel Bridge.

And Joe Bridge git too old and Jimmy McAdam bought that place. He bin take over. He was all right. Yeah, he was really kind. We were lucky, really, you know.

And then Tom Quilty take over Springvale. I learnt a lot from that katiya, the hard way. And he learnt a lot from me. I took him all over this country, showed him all the creeks and rivers. We used to go to Lansdowne robbin' cattle.

Basil I don't know. But Mick Quilty all right, I know him. Carried that young feller all over, learning him the creeks, everything. Take him out on the ride, camp out everywhere. He used to follow me. He eat crocodile. Ever eat dingo? Beautiful too, like nanny goat when you cook it. We done lot of things with him. That was Mick Quilty. And he didn't let me down. I used to go up to his place he had at Halls Creek there, little block there, sittin' out there. 'Here's a fifty.' He give me money. I bin grew him up. He gotta look after me.

I grew up all of 'em. All the kids – Charlie, then Gilbo, Finnigan, Mick. They were all mates then. Carried 'em all over the bush.

I got a wife from Moola Bulla. My two daughters born there on Springvale, down the creek near the homestead, near the moondah [paperbark] tree. Charlie born there. Gilbo born there. Right there. My biggest daughter, she's the first one that was born there. They took the one girl away from me. (*sad laugh*) She was in a school, too, you know? They just robbed 'im [her]. I had three daughters, another one died, another little girl died. I got about nine kids [now]: daughter, son, big mob.

Charlie, he bin starting learning all the talk but he bin get away too quick. He bin tooken away. They took him off from that place – Gilbo's home – just like that. That tree there, that's the place we had him. And this mob came and grabbed him. Little feller cried like hell. They bin take him to Beagle Bay then, Moola Bulla first and go to Beagle Bay after. They bin grab one child from Alice Downs, Johnny Ross. They took him too.

The missus, Olive Quilty, bin hit my daughter in the head with the shoe. I tell 'em goodbye. I take my kid away out of the school, you know. They had a school there, Quilty.

I went up to Vesty's then – Turner River. Half a year I worked there, you know, and come back to Springvale again, come back and lived there then. Then Alice Downs, not far from my home, through [the gorge] like that. Yeah. We finish up from Alice Downs, go to Turkey Creek, 'nother place.

The Chinaman Garden. Where that spring there, that's the place I started to live. Tell my wife, 'Ah, you know what we gotta do, we gotta start diggin'.' Grow some seeds, bit of a garden, you know? We had a good garden, all sort of fruit, tomatoes, and cabbage, all sort of things. Banana trees – oh, really. We used to cart the water from the creek with the yoke. One old katiya, he's there now, he find a pump. All day he patch him up, and we get manual pump to pump the water in there. And we had the water now.

No one bin there, only my wife and other old people. That's all that bin there. We muck around water carting down there. My wife didn't like it up there. She got sick and tired. Water wasn't too good, make all the people sick, you know. Good water to boil the tea with it, but bit salty. Oh, we used to drink it.

Anyway, I went further down, down where I live now and started another place there, where they built them homestead. Get them iron from the diamond mine, built all that thing up. I got a good little home there. I don't like to get away and leave 'im. I'll stay there till I die.

●

On the stations conditions for Aboriginal people varied according to individual leaseholders or managers. By the time Charlie was born there were an estimated seventy stations claiming most of the 500 000 square kilometres of the Kimberley.

Some pastoralists saw a long-term relationship with Aboriginal people as part of their tenure in the Kimberley. Several stations provided basic schooling. Others were largely indifferent to Aboriginal workers, and on some stations there was the barest regard for Aboriginal people beyond providing what was necessary to enable the station to profit. Aboriginal workers in the Kimberley were unpaid until the 1950s and did not receive award wages until the 1970s.

There was some public condemnation of treatment of Aborigines. Six royal commissions into the treatment and welfare of Aboriginal people were empowered between 1882 and 1934. No substantial Aboriginal evidence was taken by any government inquiry until the Moseley Royal Commission of 1934. Each commission identified areas of concern, including instances of maladministration by the Aborigines Department and the Police Department in some cases. Each set of findings was followed by legislation tightening the controls over the lives of Aboriginal people.

From the start policy makers were preoccupied with the increasing half-caste population. Relationships between European men and Aboriginal women, which had been tacitly sanctioned in the nineteenth century, were increasingly condemned in the twentieth as more white women moved into the area.

Successive pieces of legislation responded with increasing severity to public moral condemnation. In 1901 the Chief Protector had asked for increased powers over children of mixed descent on the grounds that 'where there are no evil influences these half-castes can be made into good useful workmen and women . . . it is our duty not to allow these children, whose blood is half-British, to grow up as outcasts and vagrants as their mothers are now'. In 1905, the Protector became the guardian of all 'illegitimate' Aboriginal children up to the age of sixteen years, with right of removal. By 1911 legislation allowed any local Justice of the Peace to send half-caste children less than eight years of age to a mission.

From 1905 Europeans, unless authorised, were prohibited from entering reserves or being within five chains (a hundred metres) of a camp. It was an offence for a non-Aboriginal man to live with Aborigines, cohabit with or travel with an Aboriginal woman. The marriage of an Aboriginal woman to a non-Aboriginal man required the written permission of the Chief Protector.

During Charlie McAdam's childhood the legislation in

place was the Native Administration Act of 1936, under which no Aborigine had guardianship of his or her child. All Aboriginal people under the age of twenty-one came under the guardianship of the Commissioner of Native Affairs, A.O. Neville, who had been Chief Protector since 1915. Aboriginal people could not move or marry without Neville's permission. They could be ordered into an institution and confined there, or ordered out of town. Cohabitation, which now included casual intercourse between Europeans and Aborigines, became a punishable offence.

Yet in 1937 Neville was expressing slowly changing public opinion when he told the first national meeting of protectors and commissioners in Canberra that the future for Aborigines lay in absorption into the dominant population through miscegenation. By 1961 assimilation of Aboriginal people would become the clearly expressed aim of federal and state government policies. While the name of the policies changed, the lives of Aboriginal people were just as regulated as they had been under the policies of protection, and a whole generation of Aboriginal children of mixed descent was removed from their families. Charlie McAdam was one of them.

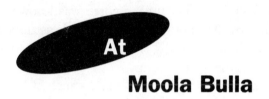

# Moola Bulla

**Charlie McAdam:**    IT MUST HAVE been 1943 or '44 the Native Affairs officer from Moola Bulla came along. We were camped under the carbeen tree near the homestead and he drove in over the rise so that we couldn't see him coming. This bloke chased me and grabbed me. I was screaming and kicking and shouting, falling down on the ground and rolling around, and my mother was crying, trying to hang onto me, but he snatched me out of her arms. I remember struggling as he tried to put these trousers onto me. I always used to wear a naga when I was a little kid, didn't know trousers until I left Springvale. In the end my mother helped put the trousers on me.

He sat me in this old car and we went straight out the main road to a place called Alice Downs, not very far from Springvale, where he grabbed up my cousin's sister's son, a feller called Johnny Ross. He was just a baby, about two years old. He was down in the creek with his mother. The same thing happened again. She was crying, he was screaming, but there was nothing you could do. He put him in the car and we went to Moola Bulla.

●

Charlie had no idea where the car was taking him. He believes that the man who picked him up was Alf George, the manager of Moola Bulla at that time. George was known as Noar, meaning 'big', by the Aboriginal people. The legislators in Perth were 2000 kilometres away. To the people on Moola Bulla, Alf George was the government.

The station complex was within walking distance of Ngar-rawarnji (Mt Barrett), clearly visible from the township of Halls Creek fifteen kilometres away. Corrugated iron and stone buildings served as the tannery, generator shed, workers' houses, garage, saddleroom, store and clinic.

In Alf George's time the clinic stocked only cough mixture, Vicks and Aspro. Further up the creek was the blacks' camp, where all the Kija people whose traditional country was Moola Bulla had camped for generations. Their half-caste children, along with the other mixed-descent children taken away to Moola Bulla, were forbidden to go to the camp. Some Moola Bulla people who had learnt particular skills and were working on the station lived in small dwellings of stone and mortar with corrugated iron roofs, sit-uated well away from the camp. Of the men, women and children removed to Moola Bulla, unmarried women and girls were locked into dormitories at night. There were men's quarters and there was a boys' dormitory, but in Charlie's day the boys camped where they could around the station complex.

The station ran cattle and sheep. There were also goats, a piggery and a vegetable garden. The men worked on all the station jobs, including sheep and cattlework, making sadd-

lery; repairs to and maintenance of yards, bores, buildings
and mechanical equipment.

The women did stockwork, cooking and cleaning. They also
milked the goats, separated the milk and cream to make butter,
and watered the vegetable garden with buckets on a yoke over
their necks. Children used to muster sheep on foot in the front
paddock, the main sheep paddock, with the women. Butter
and vegetables were reserved for the white people. Aborigines were
allowed a slice of bread and a couple of slices of boiled beef
with a mug of tea. Sugar and stick tobacco were rationed. Flour
was not provided to the Moola Bulla people living in the camp.
Mostly they lived off the land to survive, sometimes walking
miles to find game that was driven further and further away.

Some of the children at Moola Bulla, like Ernie Sara and
his sister Norma, were born there. Some had been taken there by
their white fathers. The majority were removed from the surrounding area. Families tried many ways to conceal their children
from the government agents. They rolled them up in blankets, hid them in bags, and covered them with ochre and
charcoal in an effort to hide fair skins. However officials were
assiduous in the removal of children, even searching with
torches under people's blankets in the camps at night and
taking children away while they were asleep. Paddy McGinty, a
friend of Charlie's, recalls the shock of waking up on the back of
a carrier's truck headed for Moola Bulla when he was
removed from his family at Turkey Creek.

Frank Byrne is about the same age as Charlie. He was
taken away from his mother, a Walmajarri woman, on Christmas
Creek Station, which lies between Halls Creek and Fitzroy
Crossing. His father, Jack Byrne, was head stockman on
Christmas Creek.

**Frank Byrne:**   They come there twice. The first time they
come there my mother rolled me up in a swag. But the

manager, Mac, he knew I was there and the next time they came back he came with them. So my mother, she had to let me go, like every other feller I suppose. They took me to Moola Bulla on the back of a truck, and my mother and the old feller I called Father. He was married to my mother, an old black-feller, and he was more of a father to me than the whitefeller. The whitefeller claimed me, he gave me his name, but the blackfeller was really like a father to me. He'd carry me around. He used to be the boss of the donkey dray and he made all the roads all over the place. He was a myall blackfeller but he knew what to do, how to go about these things. He'd look after all these donkeys and all the gear, he'd grease the harness all the time. That was his pride, he'd look after it.

When we first got to Moola Bulla, that old feller and my mother, they camped that night. Next morning they had me in a little place that had a fence around it. I was looking through that fence at my mother and father jumping on the truck to go away, and that's when I went crazy, to see my mother goin' away. We're not animals, we're human beings too, but they treated us like animals. I never got over being taken away from my mother. That really made my life miserable. I believe it wasn't right.

**Charlie:**  There were about 500 people there, maybe more, but Johnny and I didn't know anybody when we got to Moola Bulla. Later on we mated up with blokes like Frank Byrne, Matt Murray and Ernie Sara. It turned out that some of the people were related to me. My aunt, that was my mother's sister, was there. A feller called George Carter, a cousin of mine, was the mechanic there. He had a house, one-room house, down past the saddle shed, and he used to try and take me over to his place, but I never went. I dunno, I must have been shy. His house is still there. Same house. And there was another house next to it, where old Trooper Bedford, another cousin of mine, used to live. Doris Fletcher was there. Her husband Charlie Fletcher was a really good saddler. Old Jack Bennett, the feller who took her to Springvale, was back from the war and he was living with an Aboriginal woman called Lily, in a house there.

It was really hard on Moola Bulla. There were about thirty coloured kids there. We were hardly fed, just a couple of pieces of boiled beef and one slice of bread cut up rough. At times we used to go and pinch pigfood because we were so hungry. Every time they killed a killer they'd boil all the hoofs and guts and hide to feed the pigs, and we used to go and pinch it at night. If we were caught we'd be flogged. We used to make shanghais, just with tyre tube, a forky stick, and leather from a boot, and shoot birds and eat them.

There were no blankets. We used to sleep in the haystacks to keep warm in the winter. There was no school at the time when Johnny and I got there. We used to just wander around, camp here, camp there, camp wherever we could, and we used to get a bit of a feed, but not much.

They had no mercy on us, we had nobody to care for us, we had nobody. We were just there, to this day I don't know why. From the time that I was taken away from my mother I used to cry every night, every night, and during the day sometimes when I'd think of her. It was a really sad thing for me. Things were really hard on Moola Bulla, not only for me but for every other kid that was taken off different stations.

**Frank Byrne:** What I remember about Moola Bulla was we were like calves that got taken away from their mothers. It seems to me, now, the same thing. I had an uncle there, he's passed away now, and he was like a mother to me. I used to stop with him, and we used to camp anywhere in the creek. There were dormitories there. The dormitory, it was just a shed. Sometime you'd go there in the rain time, you know, but mainly we used to camp in the creek. Of course we used to get supplied with a blanket sometimes, but after a while you didn't see that blanket, because somebody just took it. You just lived on the best way you could.

We had meals, but the meals that we had were just the beef and bread that they put out for you, like you were a prisoner or something. All the beef they'd boil in the big boiler, and stew was made in the big boilers, and everybody used to go to a big room to get their meals. There was a kitchen there. There was a big house on the bank of the creek – they used to boil the beef and make the tea there and they used to make bread there.

When we were kids we had to be cunning or bad sometimes just so we could get a feed. They had a big boiler there. When they got a killer they'd boil up the hoofs and guts and all what people don't want to eat, and sometimes at night when we were still hungry we'd go to the boiler and have a big feed. It was rubbish, but it was something you could eat.

We used to get bullocks too sometimes. Old piker bullocks, they're old, they can't get fat. They've got beef on them all right, but they're just there, they've lived their life. They used to shoot them for the blackfellers, at the stockyards, right by the campsite where all the blackfellers were camped. We used to go and get a few feeds out of them too. We were just like scavengers. That used to be the best sort of beef we'd get, fresh beef, and everybody would enjoy that, just like a man enjoys sweets here now.

We used to spend our day like any other kids round the country but a bit different. There was nothing to do, there was no school. All of us used to play in the creeks, make little motorcars out of board, tobacco-tin wheels, and all of us used to run around in a convoy, pushing these little trucks with tin wheels, with loads on it, all going somewhere. 'We gotta go and drop these loads at *this* station.' Round and round like that.

**Charlie:**   We managed to have some good little times among us kids. We used to make little push-along wheels out of tobacco tins or treacle tins, and if we could find a piece of wood that was real neat and round, we would burn a hole through it with a wire and stick a stick through it and push it around the place, making out we were driving trucks.

In the paddock there, there's a lot of clay there. In the rainy time we used to go and get clay and make all sorts of little things out of it. We had a little pit there, and we'd make horses, or a man on a horse, all that sort of stuff. We had our good times and our bad times.

One time they were building some yards and they had all the kids barking the barks off the snappy gum trees. One morning we were barkin' the posts and we all walked off, about half a dozen of us. When they caught us we were taken into the boys' bathroom and flogged until we could hardly move. I know myself I was flogged around the back and hip and I could not walk. I crawled out of that place screaming, crying for my mother. We were crying for sympathy but we had nothing. That's how they were in those days.

One night me and Matt Murray were talking about running away from Moola Bulla. I told him, 'We'll have to go back home to my country,' that was Springvale, of course. He said, 'Yeah, I'll come with you.' In the morning we sneaked out the back and we started walking down the back road – well, it was a cart track really – that takes you back to Springvale past Five Mile Bore, or Dougall Well, they call it.

We walked and walked and walked and I don't know how, but they missed us at Moola Bulla. Alf George sent a bloke after us. Eventually we got caught about three or four o'clock that afternoon by a feller on horseback. This feller, it was either Ginger Mick or old Daylight, just stopped behind us and flogged us all the way from where we got caught back to Moola Bulla. We could hardly walk back. He pushed us all the way. We got back about seven or eight o'clock that night and he put us in this dormitory, or so-called dormitory, they had there.

Next day we had to go and see Alf George. That was another flogging, and another that night, and then we had to go and see him again in the morning – another hiding. We were flogged black and blue. I just can't explain how we felt, we were so bad.

●

Daylight, or Dick Taylor as he was also known, was one of those employed to catch and punish anyone who rebelled. He would handcuff young men or boys, tie them up and beat them with a greenhide rope or donkey chain. He regarded the katiya as his friends.

**Charlie:**   I feel sorry for that bloke now. He probably had no choice. If he hadn't flogged people, the whitefellers would've flogged him.

While I was at Moola Bulla they got rid of the sheep. They sold them to the mission at Balgo. We had to muster them all up, and a feller called Ambrose Cox, he brought some Aboriginal blokes from Balgo and then we give them a start, oh, maybe four or five mile up the road, and they kept going with them to Balgo.

We were too young to work in the stockcamp but we used to hang around the stockboys, follow them around.* Sometimes they'd chase us away with a stockwhip. We used to play at being cattle and man on a horse, take it in turns. Sometimes the stockboys let us go and catch their horses, and we used to take them down into the creek and ride them around, muddy up all the water so all the fish would stick their heads out and we'd

*Aboriginal men were referred to as 'boys' by non-Aboriginal bosses.

spear a feed. We learnt that trick from the women who used to get spinifex and get fish the same way. They'd stir up all the water, muddy it up and roll a big mob of spinifex across the top to catch fish.

Us coloured kids were not allowed to go near the camp, but every weekend at Moola Bulla all the people used to get their spears and boomerangs ready to go hunting, and we'd go too, hunting kangaroos mainly, up on Mt Barrett, Ngarrawarnji. That country used to be riddled with kangaroos before the cattle took over. It's all black soil country with red Flinders grass up to your waist, coolibah and bloodwood country. Coolibah's got a scaly grey trunk and they can grow really big. Bloodwood, he's a pink sort of tree and hard as iron. They make good yard posts. There's a yard still standing there made out of carbeen and bloodwood. Then there was one tree so soft you could carve it with a knife. The old people used to make coolamons and woomeras out of that. Of course they introduced new grasses there, that buffel grass with the brown seeds, and that silly kapok bush. It's taking over.

We used to hunt kangaroos right up the top both sides. A lot of people used to wait out on the open plain at a well called Kitchen Well – it had a windmill on it. Others would go up this hill and chase the kangaroos down to people waiting below with their spears and boomerangs and hunting dogs. What they couldn't spear the dogs would catch. This used to take just about all day. It was late in the afternoon when they used to cook the kangaroos. They used to take them to the well where there was some water, and put the billy on, and we'd eat a bit of johnny cake and kangaroo. We used to get back to Moola Bulla late in the evening.

There was a bloke on Moola Bulla, after a while, Bruno Smith. He wasn't there when I first went there, but it turned out he was my stepfather's son too, from a different woman. As far as I'm concerned he was my brother, and he claimed me as a brother too. He more or less set things up for me to go through the initiation. So I did the initiation at Moola Bulla, away from my parents, just through the people there. It was the same mob, same tribe. Kija.

The ceremonies were more or less secret. Every wet weather, when there was no stockwork, everybody used to just go bush. When they went bush each year the men used to have to take off their boots and workclothes and hand them back in at the store. We kids used to take off too. That's when we all got done. There was a big mob of us, about eight or nine of us I think.

As we got older we used to go to old Bruno Smith in the stockcamp. In the wet weather they used to cull the pikers, old bullocks that won't fatten. I used to like going out there. We used to do the tailing, riding at the back of the mob, and one day me and a bloke called Scotty Bull were tailing. I was riding a chestnut mare called Greytail and we saw this kangaroo coming down off the hill.

'Scotty! Look what's coming here!'

We chased those roos. This mare, she was a hard-mouthed mongrel. I couldn't turn her, and I'm trying to pull the stirrup out to knock the kangaroo on the head, and I got twisted up in the stirrup leather. The stirrups were too long so we used to put our foot in the leather on top of the stirrup. I was hanging half off the horse, holding onto the reins, and she galloped all the way back to the station. They caught me then. Holy suffering, didn't I get a hiding. I almost got killed.

**Frank Byrne:**  There were no working days and weekends. We had weekends all the time in fact – again, just like a mob of cattle, we just went where we wanted to, just passing the time away. When we got bigger some of us boys used to follow the stockcamp around the country. We used to walk for miles and miles. There was nothing to do. We used to just go to every bore where the stockcamp was. Me and another mate, he's at Beagle Bay now, my cousin, name of Billy Lawford, we used to go with one man Didieri up to where he was pumping water at the first bore.

Sometime when the bore was full of water, we used to walk from there now to a place west of Halls Creek. We had relations there. We used to spend a day there, then go back again, back to the bore again. It was all right. Then we used to leave him and we go back to Moola Bulla. We had to go back to the station there about once a month. The boss man, old Alf George, he used to get us around the store, and sing out everybody's name, just to make sure everyone was around the place. You'd answer yes if you were there.

Once a year everyone would take off and go into Halls Creek, the old town, for the races. Some people would go in cars but there was never any room for the kids, so us kids would walk in, all the way to old Halls Creek, and back again the next day.

There were lots of things that happened, it's a sad sort of a story for a lot of people. Some of the people used to sniff petrol. There was a man at Moola Bulla, he used to be a good feller to us, but he got onto this sniffing the petrol and he just went mad. They couldn't catch him. Without boots he could run through the hills and feel nothing. Eventually they caught him because his feet were all cut to pieces. They caught him and chained him up and put him away. But he was a good man for us, he was like a father to us until that time he started sniffing petrol. I think his name was Albert Bradshaw. Funny thing, that was the only feller that went that way. Actually they reckon that when you're sniffing that thing it's like you're in a different world, you see beautiful things and things like that.

**Charlie:** Albert Bradshaw was Pilot Murray and Matt Murray's stepfather.

I must mention this old feller, his name was Ballymungen. Now one of his kids was taken away years ago too. I've never ever met that lad but apparently he was a little coloured lad like myself. This old bloke, old Ballymungen, every night he used to take food to this house where he thought his son was. Every night he used to take some food there. It was mainly a bit of dried up old damper, or billy of tea, and a bit of meat if he had it. The old bloke used to take the food in a billy can and hang it up on the fence, and he then he would hit a wire on the fence and talk to his son.

He'd say, 'Come on, I've got tucker for you. You can come and get 'em.'

Anyway, he used to hang it up on this old fence and talk to his son, and then he'd go away. We kids would wait for him and watch him, and when he'd go back to his camp we would run over there and pinch that food and eat it all up, and put the billy can back on the fence. Poor old feller, he always thought his son who was taken away used to eat the food and leave the billy can there on the fence.

The things that happened on Moola Bulla were really bad. I've seen blokes tied around a post and flogged with greenhide ropes, flogged until they could not move. They used to tie them to a post or those bloodwood trees in front of the clinic. A couple of times there I saw blokes electrocuted, and that was really bad, you know. The saddle shed, which was the old tannery, was where they electrocuted them. They'd catch some poor bloke who was running away, or gone off with his girlfriend, something like that, and they'd chuck him in that shed with chains and handcuffs on.

●

Aborigines were sent to Moola Bulla from places as far away as Oombulgurri (Forrest River Mission), Wyndham and Beagle Bay. Some formed relationships and stayed. Others, homesick for

their country, tried to run away. They were tracked down and
brought back to Moola Bulla.

Punishments varied. When Alf George was manager of
Moola Bulla, people were given water without tea, men
were forced to wear women's dresses, or tied up and
beaten. The electrocutions were common knowledge. For
the crime of leaving the stockcamp to meet their girl-
friends, four men were chained and flogged. One was taken to
the shed, had alcohol splashed on his genitals and given an
electric shock.

Cecil Rose was the head stockman of Moola Bulla at the
time Charlie was there.

**Cecil Rose:**   I was born in Dubbo but the family shifted to
Tocumwal when I was about three. I grew up there and
worked as a ringer there, oh, I worked all over the place –
worked at St George for a while, droving cattle to Wee Waa and
Narrabri, VRD [Victorian River Downs] and other places. I
came to Moola Bulla under Alf George.

They thought I was going to be one of the floggers, but I got
on well with them [Aboriginal stockmen]. They were all good
ringers and intelligent young fellers.

Once on Moola Bulla there was no way they could leave
the joint. Ginger Mick and Daylight would track them down. A
lot of them tried. I remember one young feller got sent in
from Broome and he tried to get away. He jumped on a
donkey and rode it through a big mob of donkeys to cover his
tracks. But they tracked him. 'Hey, this one not feeding, this one
going straight.'

They used to tie the young blokes up in the loft above the
saddle shed – leave them chained up there for a couple of
days and flog them with greenhide ropes or anything that was
handy. One day a young bloke was tied up there. Alf George said
to me, 'Do you want to go and take a bit of hide off him?' I said,

'No, if I have any problems I'll deal with them out there on the flat – I'm not frightened.'

It was Snowy Dodson welded up a steel table. He used to tie them on it and put a 180 volts through it.

Snowy got burnt to death in the end, priming a carburettor with petrol over at Old Halls Creek.

**Charlie:**  The last I heard of Alf George was a story that he bought a banana plantation in Carnarvon and got wiped out by a cyclone. I don't know if it's true or not, but when I heard that story I thought, Thank God for that. Moola Bulla was a concentration camp, that's all it was.

I don't know exactly how long I was at Moola Bulla, maybe two or three years, but around 1947 they sent us to Beagle Bay.

# Broome

# and Beagle Bay

**Charlie McAdam:**    IN '47 A feller called Ernie Bridge came to Moola Bulla in a big old maple-leaf Chev truck. They loaded us coloured kids up on the back of this truck and headed off to Beagle Bay. I must have been about ten, Frankie Byrne was the same age as me, Johnny Ross would have been four or five, Keith Richards was just a baby. There were about thirty of us, girls and boys, all sitting up on the back of the truck on tins of bully beef and the rolled up swags. It was a wonder we all fitted in.

My old aunty, that was my mother's sister, was brought along too, to cook for us along the road, and another old feller, an uncle of Frankie Byrne, came along to keep an eye on us.

It was just a dirt track to Broome in those days, through Noonkanbah and Edithvale. It took three days to get there. We didn't get far the first night, just to Lamboo Station. We camped there.

**Ernie Sara:** [who was born at Moola Bulla]   For me it was the first time I was leaving my country. We didn't know where we were going. They said we were going to Beagle Bay but we didn't know where Beagle Bay was. The first night we thought we might run away, from Lamboo Station. We weren't too far from Moola Bulla, the short cut was only about twelve, thirteen miles, so we could have managed to go back. We made plans, but the old people were watching us. They kept an eye on us every night just in case we might run away, so we couldn't do anything. Johnny Cooper was from Lamboo, so he was happy when we got there.

But when we left he was crying.

●

They camped the following night at Bohemia Downs Station. The day after that the truck pulled into Christmas Creek Station. Frank Byrne thought he was going home when he saw the distant buttes and mesas rising out of the heat haze over the plain.

**Frank Byrne:**   Straight east – east of the station, you don't see it until you get right on top – the country drops. Down there is a big gorge, big gullies and things, and caves. And fish in the water, in the spring water.

At war time, before I went to Moola Bulla, they must have thought the Japanese were going to take over Australia. The same old man now, my father, the black one, they told him to load all these stores like tea and sugar, everything you've got in the store. He loaded it up into the wagon. They took it over to these caves east of the station. That's where they planted all that stuff. We hid away there for I don't know how long. (laughs) Anyway, until the Japanese went away, or they got shot, whatever they did. Then we went back home.

Anyway, we're going to Beagle Bay and we pulled up at

Christmas Creek. All sorts of things were going through my head. They drop me off here now? That wasn't the case.

Only the old feller was there, the one I called Father. He came straight to the truck and lifted me off and took me to the garden. By this time I'd forgotten all about my language, you know. Couldn't understand what they were talking about. My mother wasn't there. Unbeknownst to me, I gather that at that time my mother – she was going a bit off her head. You know how mothers worry about their kids, and she was one of them. I'm the only kid that she had. (*pause*) Anyhow, the old man, he gave me all these things – little things like a mirror and a big mob of tomatoes. He used to look after the garden too, see.

We would have been there for a little more than half an hour, or it might have been fifteen minutes, I wouldn't know. I know we weren't there too long. We went right to Beagle Bay. I don't know what happened along the way, we probably pulled up for dinner or supper or camp. The trip, I can't remember the trip. Charlie said we camped for three nights on the way.

•

World War II had a particular immediacy for northern parts of Australia after Japanese air raids on Darwin, and an air raid on Broome in 1942 which destroyed airforce planes and twelve flying boats filled with Dutch refugees from Java.

Aboriginal attitudes towards the war varied. Four hundred Aborigines, mostly from the south-eastern states, enlisted in the Australian Army. About fifty served overseas and two died in Japanese prison camps. The airforce had a number of unofficial Aboriginal units on northern airfields, and an Aboriginal navy patrol trained and carried out land patrols in the Northern Territory.

The army refused to consider arming Kimberley Aborigines, even during the fear of Japanese invasion. This was despite, or perhaps because of, a successful army training experiment on Liveringa Station in which 70 percent of an Aboriginal platoon averaged three out of five hits on a head-and-body target 400 yards away.

Many Aboriginal people thought they might be better off under the Japanese. When one man publicly expressed this view in the town of Geraldton in 1942, he was given a military escort to Moore River settlement, near Perth.

**Charlie:**   When we got to the mission at Broome we were all sorted out. We were all lined up and drafted out like a mob of cattle. A few of us stayed in Broome, mainly the older girls, who were taken to the convent to be trained as domestic servants, but the majority of us went back on the truck again and set off to Beagle Bay, a hundred miles north along a track through the pindan scrub.

•

Broome had served as a pearling lugger base from 1873 onwards. The town grew up around the mangrove flats and beaches of the bay, a haphazard shanty town of Chinese shops and gambling houses, Japanese eating houses, stores and laundries adjacent to the pubs and wide-verandahed houses of the Europeans. Aborigines camped on sandy knolls and in creek beds around the town.

Aboriginal people were the mainstay of the pearling and *bêche-de-mer* industries until the introduction of diving equipment and indentured Japanese labour. Lugger captains rounded men up on stations and marched them in chains to the coast, where they were often left on islands to be collected for diving. They were excellent swimmers, and historian Henry Reynolds has pointed out that their unpaid labour was crucial in an industry which could not have survived paying wages in its early years. The pearlers obtained fresh water, firewood, company and sex from coastal Aboriginal groups like the Bard people. In the early years many of the divers were women, but legislation in 1872 prohibited the use of women divers.

Conditions on the luggers varied. Some captains starved and beat their divers into submission. Anyone who became ill or was unfit to dive was simply put ashore at a convenient point. However, the pearling industry offered some Aborigines a greater degree of independence than station labour or domestic work. The industry attracted Chinese, Japanese and Malays, and many Aboriginal women married Asian men. European residents in Broome were disgruntled at the disruption of their labour supply brought on by the pearling industry and alarmed by the incidence of prostitution, drunkenness and venereal disease in the town. Legislators in Perth were even more alarmed at reports of a growing Asian-Aboriginal population.

The Kimberley was a frontier for missionaries as well as pastoralists and miners. The first mission at Beagle Bay, north of Broome, was established in 1890 by Trappist monks, a venture which failed after a few years due to lack of funding, a philosophical conflict between the order's contemplative ideals and the active approach required to run the mission, and disappointment at their inability to convert Aborigines.

In 1901 seven priests from the Pallottine Pious Society of Missions in Rome took over the rough timber and bark huts of the mission at Beagle Bay, and by 1907 nine nuns had arrived to help them.

Among the children sent to Beagle Bay in those years was Rudolf Newman, the son of Charlie Newman, who had the lease on Springvale Station until 1914.

**Rudolf Newman:**  I left Springvale Station in 1910 and I was just about nine years of age. Not only myself but four other kids, we left from Wyndham and we came to Broome by ship. There was no road then.

Then from here [Broome] we go to Beagle Bay in the lugger. We were sent there. At that time they had an Aboriginal protector, was a Mr Gale in those early days, and he went all over the Kimberley collecting children – every one of us coloured children. They didn't want them children to go into the bush and live like wild fellers, so they send us all up here. My father himself, he took five of us children right from Halls Creek and Springvale right up to Wyndham, driving in the sulky with the packhorses and riding horses. My mother was there too, and my uncle – old Barney, my mother's brother.

I was not taken away by force. My old father wanted to send me there because a lot of children from the Kimberley were already in Beagle Bay, boys and girls and grown-up girls, from Ruby Plains and all those places. They were all sent up there. My father wanted me to go to Beagle Bay and then after I finished my school he wanted me to go back to Springvale and look after the place because he was going to go for a holiday, I don't know where. But before he died he sold Springvale to Joe Bridge, and then he got killed riding a horse at Turkey Creek; they had races there every year. I never saw my mother again. So I got nobody. It was very strange to me, the first time when I came to Beagle Bay. The brothers were hard in those days, but you got used to it.

When the first bell rang at 6.00 a.m. we all went to church. After church we went to the breakfast and then after breakfast all the schoolkids went to school. The sisters were our teachers in those days. Then when I was about fourteen years I left school, and then I was like the master in the baker shop. I was baker there for twenty years. I worked on building the church, building houses, working in the bush, making new fences – everything I did. We used to go out hunting and things like that. Later on I had an old motorbike and I used to go all over the country on that.

They did not pay us at Beagle Bay, not that time. Later on, in the '40s, Father Frank said I had been looking after the shop for many years and he asked the archbishop to give me a bit of a salary. I was all the time working. They paid a few people then, the workers – ten shillings or fifteen shillings a week. That was it. In 1947 I went and worked in Balgo Mission. They shifted the old mission station in Balgo Hills further up and I cooked for the carpenters – good salary there.

And then from there I came here to Broome. Old man Charlton bought that bakery here, and me and old Ambrose Cox fixed it up. He got me to do it. Nobody was there to show us, and away we went until we were finished. That was about 1951. We was there for about three months and then we got it done. Me and old Ambrose Cox, he was number one builder.

Then when my father died he left some money for me, and with that money I went to Perth for a holiday for a fortnight and I come back again. And another time, in 1956, I had a good bit of money and I went to Melbourne, to Sydney and all around there, right from Sydney to Mt Isa, from Mt Isa to Darwin.

There's only one brother left now, Brother William. He came in 1951.

From 1910 I was nearly all the time there in Beagle Bay. I stayed there seventy years.

●

Missions were founded in the belief that Aborigines needed to be protected from European exploitation and the corrupting elements of white society, and that their salvation lay in conversion to Christianity. Aboriginal people accommodated the demands of the missionaries in return for a relatively peaceful existence and the provision of commodities, especially tobacco. There is evidence that the missions did ensure the survival of certain groups, and they made a significant contribution in the rudimentary education they provided to mixed-race children.

But the missions served to isolate Aboriginal people and their primary agenda was conversion through education. They were dependent to a certain degree on government funding. Government interest in Aboriginal people, on the other hand, was based on the regulation of the labour supply and the government saw the missions as eroding its authority. The pastoralists resented the missions because education made Aborigines harder to control. The missions survived because of the services they provided: food, the concentration of the Aboriginal population at certain points, and the training of people for domestic and manual labour.

During the two world wars local European opposition to the mission at Beagle Bay increased with rumours of strategic involvement on the part of the German priests. Some of the brothers were interned in Broome for a short period in World War I, and at Liverpool in New South Wales for the duration of World War II.

In contrast, the local Aboriginal people showed unprecedented support for the mission, and during that period they built the church at Beagle Bay in the style of a typical German village church, with whitewashed walls and a bell tower but constructed entirely of local material. Sixty thousand clay bricks were baked in the mission kiln. Mortar was made from sand, and crushed shells were used for lime. The frame and heavy pews were hewn from bloodwood. Hundreds of mother-of-pearl shells, all carefully graded according to size, framed the pointed windows and the paintings of the Stations of the Cross – naïve figures in bold primary colours. The symbols of the lamb, the fish and the shepherd's crook were picked out in pearl-shell tiles on the floor. The tabernacle and altar rails of bloodwood were inlaid again with Christian and Bard symbols in mother-of-pearl. The roof of beaten kerosene tins was painted blue and set with mother-of-pearl to denote the southern constellations. Giant clams formed the holy-water fonts. Thousands of trochus and cockle shells were embedded in naïve designs in the walls and altar. As Charlie says, 'There's only one way to describe that church. It's unreal.'

Some of the priests at Beagle Bay showed a scholarly interest in the culture and languages of the people. Father Ernest Worms, a German linguist and ethnologist, was parish priest of Broome from 1930 to 1938. He made a methodical study of some of the languages and culture of the Kimberley, as did Father Francis Huegel at Rockhole, near Halls Creek; and Father Herman Nekes, Professor of Linguistic and Ethnological Studies at Berlin University. Worms saw parallels in the ritual aspects of Aboriginal and Christian culture and warned against the mistake of thinking that logic necessarily operated in the same way for Aborigines and Europeans.

The post-war years saw a period of missionary expansion in the Kimberley. In 1939 the Pallottines set up a mission at Balgo Hills on the edge of the Great Sandy Desert. In 1955 they took over the running of a former government ration station at La Grange, south of Broome. Bishop Raible's successor, Father John Jobst, eventually replaced the bishop's car with a light aircraft to tour his parish.

Frank Skeen, the uncle of Evelyn McAdam (Charlie's brother's wife), went to Beagle Bay from Halls Creek straight after the war with his brother David and sister Bessie.

**Frank Skeen:**   They sent me down there to keep Teddy Bolton company. We grew up together. My father had a place called Sophie Downs, out of Halls Creek, and he was friends with old Ted Bolton, Teddy Bolton's father. I was at Beagle Bay from 1945 to 1948. Didn't do much school. They just worked us – on the farm, cutting posts with a cross-cut saw and an axe, in the carpenter's shop – I did a little bit of every-thing. They used to send us out to catch the donkeys in the mornings before school, and it would be wet and cold with the dew on the grass. We weren't used to the wet, and our feet got so cracked and sore we could hardly walk. The donkeys were just running everywhere in a big paddock in the scrub and they were hard to catch. If you got back late to school you'd get a flogging. If you didn't get the donkeys you'd get a flogging. I could never work those fellers out.

•

For Charlie, Frank Byrne, and the other children arriving on the back of the Chev truck in 1947, oblivious of the machinations of Church and West Australian State, Beagle Bay looked like just another place on the strange journey further away from their homes.

**Charlie:**   When we got to Beagle Bay, maybe two days after they drafted us out in Broome, we didn't know anybody of course. We got there one afternoon and all the local kids from the mission ran up to the truck, and they were glad to see us and they all mated up with us. Each bloke picked up a bloke as a friend, or tried to make a friend of him, and they took us to this boys' dormitory. They took the girls to the girls' dormitory.

This Beagle Bay Mission was run by Catholics. They were a Pallottine Society and they had mainly German priests and lay brothers, Irish nuns, and some Australians. It took us at least a week or so to settle in at the mission, before we started to go to school. They told me at Beagle Bay my birthday was on the 18th of December 1936, but I don't know how they knew. In those days station owners used to make a note of the birth of black kids in the station stud book, along with the foals, but I don't think my father wrote my name in the Springvale book.

When I was at this mission, for maybe the first month I still used to cry for my mother because I knew I was further away from her.

A few times there at night when I used to cry to myself,

one old priest, I forget his name now, he used to say to me, 'What are you crying for, what are you crying for young feller?'

I used to say to him, 'Oh I'm crying, I'm crying for my mother. I miss my mother.'

'Oh,' he'd say, 'go to sleep. You haven't got a mother, you haven't got a father. Go back to sleep and don't worry. You've got to go to school tomorrow morning so just go to sleep. Otherwise I'll flog you.'

Father McGinley was there when we arrived there, Father Hennessy and the old bishop, Bishop Raible, he was the Bishop of the Kimberley. There was Brother Joseph, the old feller, Brother Henry, Brother Bennett – actually there were two Brother Bennetts. Brother Pat, he came later while we were there. The nuns were Irish and Australians. Sister Katherine was our schoolteacher.

●

Father Roger McGinley went to Beagle Bay from the Pallottine house in Kew as a young man.

**Father McGinley:** It was shortly after I arrived and I remember this big truckload of children came from Moola Bulla. We were told they were orphans. Disgraceful, when you think of it. That was the Native Affairs Officer at the time. We were told that they were orphans, but they just took them away from their parents.

There would have been about ten or fifteen girls and ten or fifteen boys, give or take a few. And we were told we had to bring them up, that was all, and that was a terrible thing when you think of it now. They were just trying to turn them into white people – a disgraceful thing.

There was another thing which really disgusted me. I remember filling out the forms for child endowment and all the birthdays were the same: the 1st of April. They used different years but the birth date was the 1st of April. I thought, that's funny, they couldn't all be born on the 1st of April.

And some of the names, I don't know where they got the names from. Billy Bong – his real name was Weedon. Jack Spratt, another name. The Department of Native Affairs sent the children from Moola Bulla to Beagle Bay and they must have given them the names.

The girls were all up in one dormitory and the boys had a dormitory too. Some of the children were born there, their parents were living there, but they were in a sort of a boarding school situation. Their parents were living in the Colony and they could go there on the weekends and stay with them. It was a silly system when you think of it. We cut out the dormitory system when Father Kearney came along, later on in the '50s, and everyone lived with their parents at home.

I was there from 1947 to about 1953, six years. It was my first appointment and I did not know what I was going to encounter. Before leaving for Beagle Bay we went every Monday night to a course of anthropology lectures by Professor Adams at Melbourne University, but it was all very theoretical and it didn't help me very much when I went there. I learnt from the people. They taught me. And since then of course I've read, and tried to be open. It was beautiful in one sense when I was there. There was still a very traditional life there and nearly every night I remember they had corroborees. Our Father Worms was very much for keeping all the corroborees alive, and I remember encouraging the boys to go to the corroborees whenever we had them. And they wanted to take part in them.

Father McKelson at La Grange Mission was another one who always did everything he could to keep the culture alive. He speaks about three or four languages and he translated the Mass into Nyanamana.

That was a wonderful time. Even though we were very mis-

guided in the way we ran the place, you could say we were
children of our age. We were all misguided, we had no insight
into coping with Aboriginal affairs really. But in spite of that, I
think it was a very happy place. There were some wonderful
people there. There was the Puertallano family, there was
Annie Udgiba, a great person – she was always at corroborees,
parting her way through the smoke. And old Thomas, with
the white hair. Paddy Simplican's wife Bertha and some of the
other women used to go out fishing, and they'd come back
with magnificent white salmon and bluebone. Jackie Zohanna, I
remember him saying to me, 'Father, that Sister Katherine, she
proper chap for sums! Nobody can't beat her!' He was a very good
student, Jackie, he wrote beautiful essays and compositions. I
remember Ernie Sara, who was very good with his hands, and
Charlie. Charlie was one of the best boys there.

**Charlie:**   I remember Jackie Zohanna. His father was an
Afghan camel driver who had a place called Moonlight Valley.
Jackie's real name was Carlton. He came from a place called
Carlton just out of Wyndham. A couple of years after I left
Beagle Bay I did a couple of trips to Broome and I run into his
mother. I don't know that mob, Wyndham way, but we were just
having a yarn and an old lady said to me, 'You haven't seen
Jackie?'
   'Jackie who?'
   'Jackie Carlton.'
   'Yeah, he's in Beagle Bay.'
   'Oh, that one my own son, that one bin taken away.' It was a
sad thing. I remember talking to the old lady. 'That one was my
son.' Yeah.
   At Beagle Bay there was a divide. A lot of people were
living in houses in what they called the Colony, and then on one
side they had the camp where a lot of the old people were
living. There was no housing, just the wurleys, with a bit of iron

for the roof. I think that the Colony must have been for more educated people. They tried to separate blacks and coloureds like myself. We coloured kids were allowed to go to the Colony, but except for the kids whose parents were living in the camp we weren't supposed to go near the camp. We used to spend time with the people though. One old feller, old Thomas, had been at the mission a long time. He used to tell us stories about working on the pearl luggers before he came to Beagle Bay.

After a while I met a relative of mine there, my mother's brother. I remembered that my mother told me, a long time ago before we were taken to Moola Bulla, 'If you go to Beagle Bay Mission you go and see one old man there, his name is Medawinjun.' Medawinjun was a very close relative of my mother. He and Aunt Lily were taken away to Beagle Bay before I was born, at the time Rudolf mob went, and he was the only person that me and Johnny knew when we got to Beagle Bay. I asked around for him, but I didn't know his white name was Paddy. The other people used to call him Tjunga Tjunga Paddy, that means Chain Paddy, because he used to be a police tracker.

I asked around for him, and people would say, 'No, who's that? We don't know him.' And I said, 'He's here in Beagle Bay somewhere.' Eventually I was talking to the old feller himself and he said, 'Where you come from – Springvale?' And I said, 'Yeah.' And he said, 'You're Burrel's son! Yeah, you're my kid, you're my relation.'

'You Medawinjun?' I asked him.

'Yeah,' he said, 'that's me.' It might have taken me a week or a fortnight to find him, maybe a month, I just forget now. He was the only bloke that me and Johnny knew. Well, we didn't know him, it was just that my mother told me, 'When you go over there, you'll find him there.' And he was still there. He continued my education a bit, but actually I lost some of it after a while because I was away from my country.

Some of the priests, not Father McGinley, told us that we had to forget our culture. They said we couldn't believe two things at once. We were allowed to go to corroborees but not take part in them. Some of the priests were interested in our culture. One old feller, Father Rutherford, used to take me everywhere. Me and Johnny Ross used to go to the guest house where he was staying and he used to ask us different words in lingo. What do you call kangaroo in lingo? What do you call this and that? And we used to tell him. He'd write it down. I remember talking to him. He used to ask us different questions, because I think he was interested in that. He was the son of a famous woodcutting family.

Actually we had better times at Beagle Bay. At least we used to get three feeds a day, and we could feed ourselves if we got hungry and when we were away from the mission. There was a lot of wildlife there, kangaroos, wallabies, fish, and all sorts of bush fruit. We used to shoot birds with shanghais, mainly doves and that, and ducks, and we used to cook them and eat them and all that sort of thing.

We used to go to school and have a good time with the kids. They gave us a little uniform to wear, just a shirt and shorts. They used to get bags of secondhand clothes sent up from Perth. We had a different shirt to wear on Sundays for what they called our Sunday clothes, and at Christmas we'd get a new shirt too. We used to have our own little games, a sort of football, and Beagle Bay rules hockey, and all that sort of thing. We used to have our school sports, and we used to go out to the beach, do a bit of fishing. The nuns did all the teaching in school and the brothers taught us about different trades. Saturday was chore day and we used to go around picking up rubbish all over the place.

It wasn't too bad at all, but the brothers, mainly the lay brothers and some German priests, they were very cruel. Any little thing you'd do, you'd be flogged for. If you pinched an apple or went into the kitchen and pinched a piece of bread or something, you'd be flogged. The mission kept a mob of donkeys for carting firewood. If we were caught riding those donkeys, we'd be flogged. And I mean flogged too. They'd flog you until you'd be screaming, shouting, carrying on, and then they'd tell you to go.

I remember Brother Henry. He was cruel, that guy. Someone reported kids riding donkeys. There was Frankie Byrne, another kid called Ralphie Rivers, and one other feller. I don't know which kid reported the other kids for riding those donkeys, but they reported these poor kids to this Brother Henry. That evening we went to the dining-hall where we used to eat and Brother Henry walked in there. Brother Henry grabbed those three fellers and flogged them. There was nothing they could do about it. We couldn't do anything, we were only kids, and the grown-up men did nothing. I don't know if they were afraid of him. The nun that was there cooking that night, she never said a word.

That night, after these poor kids were flogged, we went back and told the priest there. I just forget who the priest was. All he said to these poor kids was, 'Look, that's your own fault, you shouldn't be riding donkeys.'

You know, they didn't have sympathy towards kids there. The priests did nothing to stop kids getting bad hidings like that. We always got the blame.

In Beagle Bay I was punished one time. I never knew what for, I don't know whether I swore, or whether there was a fight with somebody, or misbehaving in school. To this day I don't know what I did, but I know I was locked up for two days and one night in the building joining the little boys' dormitory we used to live in. There was a little room on the end and it just had a little manhole on top to get in, you couldn't get out of it because there were bars there. They used to bring bread and beef over to me. No tea, just water. I often think about that, because you know I was only a young lad and I didn't do anything criminal, but I still got locked up for two days and one night. Those are some of the things that happened in Beagle Bay. I'll never forget that.

There's another story I'd like to tell, about using the toilets. It was a brother called Brother Pat. Anyway, Brother Pat was looking after the kids, us mob now, and one time I can remember I had diarrhoea, I got short taken, and I used his toilet.

A day later he called me over to his house and he said, 'Charlie, where did you go to the toilet the other day?'

I said, 'Oh, I don't know, Brother.'

He said, 'Yes, I think I know where you went. Is this your belt?'

I couldn't deny it because it had my name on it. I said yes.

He said, 'You know where I found this?'

'No.'

'You know all right where I found this. I found this in my toilet.' He got hold of a strap and flogged me for using his toilet. I wonder what would have happened if I had squatted to go to the toilet behind one of the oleander bushes there. No matter what I'd done I was doing something wrong, and if I were to do it behind those oleander bushes I probably would have got half killed again, so there was nothing to it. It didn't matter much – whichever way it went I still would have got a hiding. You couldn't win there.

Brother Pat didn't stay long at Beagle Bay. He was only there for a short while before he contracted leprosy and had to go to the leprosarium in Derby. Actually I met him in Kew the other day when I went to see Father Roger McGinley. I hadn't seen him since way back in 1950.

When we got to know our way around we met up with some of the bigger boys. There were a few blokes there from Halls Creek – Frank Skeen, Teddy Bolton, David Skeen, and Johnny Skeen.

We used to have problems with some of the bigger boys. Grown-up men they were, most of them. They had their own dormitory. There used to be a big boys' dormitory and a little boys' dormitory. These big boys used to bully us to do things for them, to go and get them a drink of water, or to go and ask someone for a cigarette, things like that. If we refused we'd get slapped in the face or something like that. I suppose we put up with it.

Every now and then, we kids used to chase the old blokes at the Colony to frighten them. We used to bark these gum trees and make a bark boomerang from them. They were fully grown men, in their thirties and forties and that, and we used to cut a big mob of barks and give them a few, and we'd have a few, and we'd have a good old fight. Every time we used to fight these old fellers we used to come out on top. They thought us blokes from Moola Bulla were myalls and didn't know any-thing about fighting with boomerangs, but they got a big shock because we learnt all that sort of thing when we was kids back at Moola Bulla. And I learnt a bit of that stuff at Springvale and the other lads, they probably learnt all that sort of thing wherever they came from. So the men got a very big surprise. Sometimes we used to hurt them and they'd chase us with real boomerangs and try to get stuck into us, but we were a bit too quick for them and we used to run away from them. It seems funny now, but it wasn't funny at the time because those boomerangs used to hurt, really hurt, and if they hit you they could knock your eyes out or break your arm or wrist or something like that because they were really hard. One of those old blokes chasing us with a real boomerang would get rid of us straight away.

One thing about Beagle Bay, I remember they had a beautiful garden there. Brother Henry used to run it. They used to grow everything there. There were banana trees, coconut palms, watermelons, rockmelons, cabbages, lettuces, tomatoes – all sorts of things. When the watermelons and rock-melons used to ripen up, and the tomatoes, we used to go and pinch them at night. Sometimes we used to get caught, sometimes we didn't.

But I must tell you this funny story. I thought only us kids used to go and pinch the stuff from the garden, but the old blokes from the Colony used to go and pinch stuff from there too. One night, about three or four of us were in there pinching tomatoes, crawling in between the tomato bushes. They used to have a V-shaped trellis made of sticks to grow the tomatoes on, and we crawled in underneath it and started feeling these tomatoes, seeing if we could find a ripe one. Everything there was so quiet. Anyway one old bloke from the Colony was there doing the same thing from the other end, crawling underneath the trellis trying to find ripe tomatoes. One of the lads, I think it was Ernie Sara, he and this old bloke were crawling towards each other from different ends of the garden and they bumped heads in the dark. Ernie thought he'd bumped into a ghost and there was a hell of a commotion, and blokes going in every direction. This old bloke was running back to the Colony and we're running back to the dormitory.

Next morning we were still laughing about it, but I'm glad those old blokes from the Colony didn't know who the lads were in the vegetable garden, because they probably would have given us a hiding too. Nobody knew what we were laughing about. It was good though.

One afternoon there was a goat in the mission garden and about three or four of us boys tried to get it out of there. We chased it round and round, and in the end I stuck my foot through the end of a bottle. I almost cut my toe off. It was pretty sore, so I went to the hospital and they stitched it up for me and bandaged it all up. But a couple of days later it must have got infected. I couldn't walk for about two weeks, I just lay there in pain. I was really crook, I couldn't eat or anything. The priest used to come over and say a prayer over me. They couldn't do much for me. In those days I don't know what they had in the hospital. I thought I was going to die at one time there, but I survived it.

On the funny side of things now, there were two fellers called Raymond Clements and Aloysius Charlie. The girls used to be locked up in their dormitory but the boys weren't locked up, and the big boys had a separate dormitory. Sometimes at night one of the boys would sneak around to the girls' dormitory and talk to their girl though the window. This Aloysius Charlie, he was one of those blokes who liked to have a bit of fun. One night he borrowed a white sheet off someone and ran around to the girls' dormitory. He knew Raymond was going over there to see his girlfriend. So when Raymond was talking to his girlfriend through the dormitory window, Aloysius Charlie walked around the corner with this white sheet around him and clapped his hands.

When Raymond Clements saw this white figure coming towards him he thought it was one of those nuns and he cut it. He jumped a six-foot fence, but on the other side of the fence there was a well full of water and Raymond fell straight into the well. It was not deep because the water table is pretty close to the surface in that part of the country, but it was freezing cold.

Aloysius ran back to the dormitory – it wasn't very far – and took the white sheet off him. We were all sitting there, and up comes Raymond about twenty minutes later, all soaking wet. The blokes all jumped up. 'Hey, what happened to you?'

'Oh,' he said, 'I just went to the toilet. When I walked around the corner of this building here I slipped into the swimming-pool.' We used to have a swimming-pool by the dormitory there, the boys' dormitory.

Aloysius said to him, he said, 'Hey, don't bullshit, mate.' He said, 'You were sneaking out of the dormitory and you got chased, didn't you?' Raymond didn't know what to say. So everybody was teasing him and it was really really funny. In the end I thought Raymond was going to kill poor Aloysius Charlie. Everybody laughed about it that night, and all next day they teased him. It was so funny the way Aloysius Charlie told the story.

We used to like getting away from the mission. There was an old feller, a lay brother, called Mr Sachs who lived about five miles from the mission towards the beach. He had a little garden there and the pearlers used to come in to get their water and provisions from him. One of the jobs we boys had was to load up the donkeys with meat and stores and take them out to him. That used to be a good day.

We had good times hunting and fishing at Beagle Bay. We used to go and catch wallabies with the box wires that used to be wrapped around fruit boxes that were sent to Beagle Bay. We used to get that wire and put a loop in it and set it up at night on kangaroo tracks where they used to go in for water, sometimes along the fence. We'd go and set them at night and early in the morning we'd go to see what we'd caught. We'd catch quite a few too, just quietly.

Sometimes I used to go out hunting wallabies with Rudolf Newman. He used to be the baker, and if we caught a wallaby he'd cook it in the big oven.

On moonlight nights we used to go and catch eels. We used to go out and see them crawling around and we used to knock them on the head. We'd have to be very careful because it could have been a snake crawling around. Otherwise we would put a fishing-line down their hole and catch a few like that, with a frog for bait. Some of the eels would be about two foot long so we used to cook them up and have a good old feed.

In August they used to have what they called a retreat. The priests and the brothers, for this month they don't talk to anybody, and when they pray in the church they don't voice the prayer.

That's when we used to go for holidays, out to the seaside, to places like Midlagoon and Balkajok. We used to always have a priest there with us to look after us, and a couple of cooks. My favourite place was Midlagoon. We were supplied with fishing-lines and our little swag, and we'd stop there for fourteen days, or however long it took for the retreat to finish.

One year we went on a camping trip with Father McGinley. We had a little wagon, driven by about six or seven donkeys, to carry our blankets and a little bit of tea and sugar and flour. We went to a place called Weedong. Everybody used to talk about how good Weedong was, they used to say there were big lakes and plenty of water there. When we got to this place Weedong, there was no water. The bore wasn't pumping, the lake was dry. We were there for a couple of days and we thought we were going to perish. The first two mornings that we were there we had to suck leaves to get a drink, because there used to be a heavy dew and the leaves were very wet. I think that's what saved us.

A few of the boys went looking for water about ten miles further up. I think there was another bore there, and they were very lucky to find water there for us. We had no containers, we only had billy cans, so they had to put the water in the billy can and bring it back to Weedong. We were there for about a week, and a couple of boys used to go in the wagon and cart water about ten miles in billy cans. The priest, Father McGinley, was amazed at what we knew about bush life, even though we were little kids. We could have all perished to death, we had no contacts, no radios, no nothing. But we got back safe to Beagle Bay in the end.

We had some good times when we used to get away from the mission because we were just about running wild. No, it wasn't too bad in Beagle Bay.

**Father McGinley:** Midlagoon. That's one thing that will stay in my mind all my life. I remember one day, I said, 'Now go out and look for shells and I'll give a prize for someone who brings back the biggest shell and someone who brings back the smallest shell.' I was amazed at the ability of those girls and boys to find things, because someone came back with an enormous shell, and someone came back with a little thing no bigger than your smallest finger-nail, a tiny little shell, perfectly formed – beautiful. And then we found a huge turtle. Mother Agnes cooked the turtle and it was beautiful. We found turtle eggs on the beach and we cooked them too.

The year that we went to Weedong was the first time I had ever been on a mule, and the boys had a great laugh at Father's sore backside.

I was constantly amazed at the knowledge of those boys and girls, and their tremendous bush sense – an ability to see and hear a long way away. Bush fruit, they could see it a mile away. And they would remember. I remember once we went out for a picnic, and someone said, 'Oh, this tree, last year, we found a barney here.' Things like that. And it would be the exact spot, the exact tree, where they had found something the year before. That sense of being at home in the bush is a wonderful gift, I think.

**Frank Byrne:** I've got nothing against Beagle Bay. It was good for us. I didn't learn much, but school was all right. Sister Katherine was our schoolteacher. She was nice. I wasn't any sort of a scholar at school but I could read and write and add up sums and all that. Not many of our people learnt those things in those days. They taught us how to manage, and to respect the elder people. If you didn't show respect, then they'd give you a good hiding. We used to have plenty of prayers – we used to pray before we'd start school and pray again before we left in the afternoon. We used to be altar boys and we used to pray in Latin. We'd say the Latin words. We could just about say the Latin as well as the priests but we didn't know what we were talking about.

When we started to go to school we were put to work too, mainly gardening, carting the goat shit to the garden. There was a big mob of us, some coming and some going back with a little bag of goat manure, just like ants. They had all sorts of things, you could be whatever you wanted. You could be a butcher, you could be a mechanic, you could be a gardener, you could be anything. Sometimes we used to do the shit run – don't know a nice way to say it – everybody used to have a go at that, might be Friday or whenever.

An old feller named Casimah was the boss of that. He was a good old man. He and another bloke there named Boney Doonbah used to play the flute. Boney was local. Richard Cox was another one. He was an old carpenter. He wasn't an ordinary carpenter at all. He used to make beautiful guitars. They were self-taught, those blokes, they were always mucking around with music, and the hymns they would sing in Latin.

That place was just musical. It was picked up from the priests, the German priests. The Australian priests weren't much of singers. They used to play the organ, and the priests used to sing the Mass, and the girls and blokes answered the prayers in songs. It sort of makes me feel sorry when I hear that today, we used to sing it too. The choir was terrific, it was unique.

The brothers were good, but when they gave you a hiding they really gave you a hiding. One old feller, Brother Henry, was a very dangerous man. Sometimes we used to ride donkeys, and this is what happened when I was working there in the kitchen. Some boys would sort of take turns working in the kitchen. Anyway, that day we rode some donkeys. Brother Henry came with the strap for the sewing-machine, the little steel strap – they hurt very much, those little fellers – and he flogged me and flogged me.

Everyone used to get a hiding for that, because the donkeys would do a lot of work, carting wood on the drays and all those things, and the kids wouldn't let the poor things have a spell – they'd just jump on and gallop them all day. We could all ride, with just a stick, no bridle. You'd jump on them with nothing, just a little long stick, and to turn the donkey that way you'd hit him over on one side, and then hit him on the other side to turn him back. And as well we used to cut a little short stick and poke him in the back and make him gallop faster. We were pretty good riders, we had pretty good balance.

At Beagle Bay every weekend we'd take our fishing-line out, and a little billy can, tea and sugar, and go fishing – and that's how we used to feed ourselves on weekends. We used to catch all sorts of fish, barramundi – we used to call them skipjack, not barramundi – flathead, rock cod. And the perch fish – we used to call it bluebone because it had blue bones in it.

We used to spear stingray. To cook it you just chuck it on the flame. It doesn't cook at all, you just singe it and turn it over a few times. When you pull it out you cut off the little wings or flaps on both sides, and then take the fat out of the stomach. Stingrays have a lot of fat in the stomach and you eat that raw with that flap. You wouldn't believe it but it's nice. Sometime we used to fry it too, but it doesn't taste so good when you fry it.

There were all sorts of shells. Scallops, periwinkle – or long bum, whatever they call it – and little snails that live on top of the mangroves, and others that live in sand on the beach. We used to dig them out and cook them too, they're nice. And the crabs. We used to spear a big mob of crabs in the gullies around the mangroves. I don't think there were as many crocodiles in those days. We never used to bother about them really.

It was then, while I was at Beagle Bay, my mother died. I would have been about ten. Father McGinley, he's the one that told me my mother had passed away. He never tell me where. I've got an idea – you know the way people talk, you can gather bits and pieces here and there – that she went to Perth, to what they call the asylum there.

Later on when I went back to Christmas Creek and Halls Creek I asked where she was buried. Nobody tells me. I wanted to go to the grave and see where it was, but nobody tells me where it was. It was the same for the old feller that was married to my mother, nobody told me where he was buried either. I went back to Fitzroy Crossing to see my old uncle there, Uncle Jock Stanley, and he never told me anything. That's the reason now that I'm crooked on the government, and I'll say it again. They took me away from my mother, and I don't care who he is, every person, every human, they have this thinking about their family. My mother was like that, might have gone mad worrying about me, what sort of things were happening to me, that's probably why she went that way. I was the only kid she had.

I used to think about her all the time and – this is unbeknownst to anybody else – I used to be on my own and I'd cry for my mother. Even today I'm still not right. A lot of people tell me I work too hard, but I do that because that's all that makes me feel right.

●

Frank Byrne left Beagle Bay before Charlie, when he was about fourteen. They met again, and worked together on a number of stations in the Northern Territory, but the first time Frank ever spoke to Charlie of his mother's death was in Alice Springs in 1994.

**Charlie:** Anyway, the years went on, and I always wanted to get back to find my mother, back to Springvale Station. I think it was in 1951 or '52 that I got kicked out of the mission.

I said to Johnny Ross, 'Johnny, you know what? I'm going to go back to my country.'

He said, 'They won't let you go.'

I said, 'Yes they will. I'm going to cause trouble.'

He said, 'How you going to cause trouble?'

I think I was about fifteen. Anyway, I had a girlfriend. Actually my first sexual experience was with a nun, a beautiful little Irish colleen. I didn't know what was going on at first, but she showed me. The nuns were just girls not much older than us, and when the older nuns would go on their retreat down to the coast some of them would stay behind.

Later on we used to sneak over at night to the girls' dormitory, and this place used to have a paperbark roof. We used to lift the roof up and slip under it into the girls' dormitory. One night I made a big commotion and got caught.

Father Jobst, he's a bishop now, was the priest that kicked me out of the place because I was misbehaving. The reason I was misbehaving was I knew that was the only way to get out of that place.

He told me that I was a wicked man and I was in my glory. I said to Johnny, 'No worries, Bruz, I got kicked out. I'm going back home, I'm out of here.'

That was the start of an adventure for me. Father Jobst kicked me out and I got a lift to Broome. All I had was my singlet and shorts, and the shorts were pretty well hanging by threads, they were torn here and there. I knew nobody when I got to Broome. I tried to find an old lady called Aunty Gracie but I couldn't.

I managed to get a job on a cargo boat taking water and food out to the pearling luggers, and I was seasick the whole time. At the end of a week they paid me £3 10s. All I wanted to do was get to Halls Creek so I could go back to Springvale.

# Back
## to Springvale

**Charlie McAdam:**  I GOT A lift out of Broome with a
truckie, but we broke down not very far from Derby at a
place called Langey Crossing, across the Fitzroy River. So I
had to turn around and get a lift back into Broome. A week later
Father McGinley came into town with some fellers in the
Beagle Bay Mission truck on their way to Balgo. They were
pleased to give me a lift, and Father McGinley gave me a
blessing.

I hitched another ride from the Balgo turnoff into a place
called Rockhole, about fifteen mile from Halls Creek. An old
hawker called Joe Williams used to have a little shop there at
Rockhole. I asked Joe if I could get a lift to Halls Creek and he
said, 'Yeah, no worries,' so I stopped with him. He gave me a
feed and looked after me for couple of days or so, and he
gave me a lift to Halls Creek.

When I got to Halls Creek I went looking for an old Irishman
who used to own the store there, a very nice old person called

George Burke who knew my father Jimmy McAdam very well. I told him who I was, and he said straight away, 'Ah, what, do you want to go back to Springvale?' And I said yeah and he said, 'All right, I'll send a telegram and see if I can get Tom Quilty to pick you up.'

Sure enough next day Tom Quilty sent his son over, Mick Quilty, to pick me up. Mick was just a kid at the time.

●

Charlie's father had sold the Springvale lease to Tom Quilty in December 1948. The son of Irish immigrants who had settled in Queensland, Quilty was already a substantial land holder. The lease which he held with his brother Paddy on Bedford Downs, adjoining Springvale, comprised over a million acres. Tom Quilty was something of a bush poet, his poems revealing a sentimental side and a drinking habit. He was also legendary for his horsemanship. Tom was sixty-one years old when he purchased Springvale and went to live there, ten years after Paddy's death from appendicitis. The deal on Springvale included 5000 cattle and 100 horses. It was said that while Tom complained for years about the price of £17 000 he had paid for Springvale, he mustered enough cleanskins, or unbranded cattle, off the place to pay for it in the first year.

When Charlie stepped out of the car at Springvale there was an emotional reunion. The whitefeller population might have changed, but the Kija population by and large had not. Only Warragunye was not there: the old man who had eluded police raids and avoided confinement on Moola Bulla had fallen ill in the end and died in the Native Hospital in Wyndham. Charlie's mother and the rest of his family were still there, as were his jimari Rusty Peters and his family. Rusty's father was head 'boy' in the stockcamp.

**Charlie:** That was when I first found my mother again. My sister, my old grandparents, my Uncle Yunguntji were all there at Springvale. When they saw me and I saw them, we all started to cry. We cried and cried – cried with joy, I suppose. We had no contact over the years. They did not know whether I was alive and I didn't know whether they were still alive. My mother just could not believe I had come back to her. Poor old thing – she picked up a rock and hit herself and laid her arms open in the way the old people did. That was my happiest day. I couldn't get over it.

My sister was there. She had had a kid from Clifton after a while, a lad called Clancy, a great little feller, but he got sick and they sent him away to Perth. And he never come back – died. She had another boy, and then she ended up living with a feller called Sammy Calywyn. He was a smart man, that feller Sammy. They had about four kids – two boys, two girls, I think. Rusty Peters was there. He was not taken away because he was full-blood.

I also found I had a brother called Gilbert – Gilbo. Not long before I was taken away to Moola Bulla I remember a young woman came walking down the road into Springvale. She was just a girl really. She became Gilbo's mother. Her name was Mingalkil – or Jeannie, the whitefellers called her. The Quiltys brought another young kid when they came from Coolibah, a young feller they called Finnigan Quilty, and they had him and Gilbo; Clancy and Russia Clifton; Rammel Peters, who was Rusty's brother; and Yunguntji's daughters, all living up at the homestead.

I started working at Springvale for five bob a week. It was hard work too, from daylight till dark. My first job was cleaning the stockyard, cleaning out all the cow dung and that sort of thing. I used to have an old tin steel-wheeled wheelbarrow and I used to have to push it across a little sandy creek there. You can just imagine trying to push a steel-wheeled wheelbarrow through sand. That went on for a while until the mustering season started.

Every year the mustering season used to start up in March. Before that, at horse muster time, we used to muster the horses up. Rod Quilty, Tom Quilty's son, was head stockman in those days. His other son Basil took over later when Rod went to manage Lansdowne. Rod Quilty gave us three horses each to get ready for mustering. We always shod our horses, especially round Springvale. Even in the soft country in the Northern Territory you can't work horses, chasing cattle and that, without shoes on, because once you start galloping they get tender very quickly. That's what I've found anyway.

When we finished shoeing the horses we rode out to the stockcamp and did the mustering from there. We never came back into the homestead in the mustering season. We were always out at one stockcamp or another, just moving from one mob to the next mob. The day would start around four o'clock in the morning, depending on the job we had to do. In the summer we'd be up about three, and in the winter it might be four, maybe five o'clock. It all depended on the weather and what we had to do that day. At four o'clock in the morning there's no moonlight, it's dark then. By the time we'd get the horses back it would be five or six in the morning. I reckon the furthest we'd go from the stockcamp would be about fifteen miles before we'd start to muster. In bullock muster time we had to follow their tracks, because bullocks walk a long way to feed – fifteen miles, easy. Once we caught up to them they might all be galloping bastards, so we had to settle them down and by the time we got back to camp it might be five or six o'clock in the evening, easy. That happened to me lots of times. It could be eight or ten o'clock at night when we'd finish. Sometimes we worked fifteen- or eighteen-hour days.

At other stations where I worked after Springvale, each

man had four horses: three mustering horses and one what they call a cutting horse, or camp horse. But on Springvale we had three horses each: a stock horse, a camp horse and a bronco, or roping horse. Sometimes you would muster all day, and get the mob back to the stockcamp by three, maybe four o'clock. Then for the last three or four hours of the afternoon we would tail the mob out, just hang onto them until they settled down on the camp for the night, and we might not change horses that day.

If we mustered until dinner time [lunch] and came back about two o'clock, there would be time to have a bit of a feed, and then you'd change onto your cutting horse. The rest of the afternoon you'd be cutting strangers out, or cutting all the bullocks off, to put just the cows and calves through the yard. We'd let the bullocks out, and then next day we would start branding and we used our bronco horses for that. Branding might take half a day, a full day, whatever. It just depended on how many cattle we had in the yard. Branding two or three hundred head of calves would probably take all day. If we knocked off branding early there was always something else to do, a little short muster for that afternoon to get ready for next day, something like that. Say if we finished about two o'clock, we'd get fresh horses and then go out about ten miles to muster for the next day. Never a dull moment, I tell you. It's different these days. Now they got helicopters and Toyotas and motorbikes.

We used to have yards near the main station, but when we used to go mustering out from the stockcamp we never had yards. We used to bring them all the way back into the stockcamp, back to the bore, or wherever we were camped. There was no such thing as portable yards. In those days we just drafted them out of the mob with a camp horse.

That was a good horse, the camp horse. Tom Quilty had a very smart horse called Bemi, a beautiful camp horse. Tom would take the bridle off and ride him in the camp just with a rope around his neck. He would flick the back of the beast he wanted, just one stroke of the whip, so Bemi would know which beast it was, and that horse would cut out that beast all by himself, with Tom Quilty just sitting there. When that horse died, old Tom buried him on Springvale next to the graves of his wife's parents.

Every bloke had a different taste in horses. My father had thoroughbreds on Springvale, but Tom Quilty decided to have Arabs because he reckoned they were tougher working horses. And then, if I can remember rightly, he had these Arab mares crossed with some thoroughbred stallion he bought from New Zealand, then he crossed them back to an Arab. I suppose he was trying to get the toughness and the speed. That's just my way of thinking. I never asked him or anything like that.

They had some good horses. They had thoroughbreds they used to cross with Clydesdales as well, so they could have the size and a little bit of speed. If they threw more towards the Clydesdale they would break them in for bronco horses, to pull the calves and catch bulls and all that sort of thing. I reckon that was a good breed because they were big solid horses that could do anything.

For branding and cutting we used to use bronco horses, or maybe mules, they're good workers. Two blokes on bronco horses with lassos would ride in amongst the cattle and throw a rope on a beast, then drag 'im off to the bronco panel. Once you put him in a bronco panel then you've got him, and all you do is put two leg ropes on the calf, front and back, knock the panel down, brand him and castrate him. We used to race. Say there were two blokes on bronco horses, we'd be racing to be the best bloke on a bronco horse. Or if we were on the ground leg roping, we'd be racing to see who was the best leg roper. That was good fun, we used to enjoy that. I reckon in a good day we did about three hundred head, easy, because we had to pull up for lunch and give the poor old bronco horses a spell for a couple of hours, and then back to the yard again. That was it. It was good. Next morning we'd let the cattle out and we'd do the same thing all over again.

It was a hard, tough job. It used to keep you fit, really fit, and we didn't have very much to eat in the stockcamp. We lived on dry corned beef and damper. All we had was flour, sugar and tea-leaf, maybe a bit of golden syrup or treacle. We were very, very lucky if we had any onion or rice or something like that. When the corned beef ran out and we got a killer, we reckoned we were having a feast – it was like Christmas. We used to salt the majority of the meat and boil it up in big bowls.

Some stations employed a cook on the stockcamp, but with old Tom Quilty you never had a cook. We used to go in turns, me or Basil or some other blokes. You'd knock off early, say, maybe five or six o'clock, put a damper on and put a bucket of corned beef on, and boil up. Corned beef and damper, that was it. And tea. Old Tom Quilty used to have half a teaspoon of epsom salts in his tea, every time. He reckoned it was good for his system. No spuds, no onions in those days. Breakfast in the morning, same thing. Cup of tea, cold corned beef and damper. No lunch during the day unless we were lucky, but usually we came back to camp too late. This went on year in and year out. We really got used up, us young fellers. I was in my teens then.

The kids used to work with us too. There was my young brother Gilbo McAdam, he would have been eight or nine; Rammel Peters, he was only a lad not even in his teens; young Russia my nephew, and Finnigan Quilty. They used to work like men, up at three in the morning, saddling up their horses – didn't matter if it was cold or not. The kids had no shoes. Tom Quilty wouldn't buy shoes for them because he reckoned they were too small to wear boots. The poor little buggers. What used to make me sorry, and I still think about it today, was that they used to eat dry damper and corned beef and they weren't allowed to drink tea. If they could they used to sneak over to the old blokes, the round-up blokes, to get a cuppa tea off them to wash their food down. Those kids, you know, they used to work like men and they'd get abused by Tom Quilty or Basil Quilty, because they expected things from them that they expected of grown men. The Quiltys treated them like grown men and yet they were little kids. I'll never forget that.

After tea in the stockcamp we just rolled out our swags and fell asleep. In those days a swag was a piece of canvas, say eight foot by ten foot wide, with a couple of blankets rolled up with a leather strap – not a big warm rubber swag like you have today. They had to be a reasonable size because the pack-horses couldn't carry too much weight. There were about six packhorses to carry, say, ten swags and the stores, and some of those old mules used to take only two swags. Your pillow was a pillowcase with your clothes stuffed in it, and we used to roll that up in the swag. Actually sometimes we used to use our saddle-cloths for blankets when it was too cold. They're only about a metre square, those checked saddle-cloths, but we used to chuck it over ourselves to keep our shoulders warm.

It's got me beat how we used to survive, for lots of reasons. We never worried about snakes when we rolled out our swags, but there's heaps of death adders, king browns, everything in that country.

A bruise or a cut was nothing out in the bush. If you got a deep cut and you were round about a bloomin' itchy grub nest, you put that on it and it swells up and stops the bleeding. It's a horrible sensation but those itchy grub bags can save your life. It irritates the skin terrible – you feel like scratching it or getting a knife and cutting it off. Once it falls on you, in seconds it just swells up. That's why they put it on the wound, because it tightens everything up and stops the bleeding. It's a bastard to bump into but it's a nice thing to have out in the never-never.

When I think back, we used to chase bullocks or cows or calves flat out and never think what would happen if the horse put his foot in a hole. In fact in 1953 or '54 Rusty Peters' father was killed at Rosie's Yard when he was cutting out a Springvale beast from the Flora Valley cattle. He chased it between two little kungka berry bushes and someone had left some barbed wire laying there, and the horse he was riding got tangled up in the barbed wire and fell on him. Rusty's family left Springvale not long after that.

It's funny, young people today won't believe that you can jump onto a three- or four-year-old bull and pull him by the tail and hold him down. Just the other day I was at Love's Creek giving them a hand with the bullocks and these young fellers reckoned they couldn't hold one. So I got up and pulled him down and they all said, 'Jees, how'd you do that?' It's just a knack of pulling them at the right time, pulling them when they're turning, and they fall flat on their back. You get him by the tail and you sort of wrap it round your wrist, or hand. Soon as he turns, you pull. He'll always turn towards you and when you give him a pull at the right time, the way he's turning, you can flick him fair on his back. Then when he falls you grab him by the leg, or put the tail between the leg, and hold him up so someone can come and give you a hand.

Young fellers say, 'How'd you do that? You must still be strong!' It's not a matter of being strong, anyone can do it. It doesn't matter how big a bullock is or how old he is, you get hold of him and the moment he spins around to charge you, you pull him, and you don't have to pull hard, just a quick flick will do it, and he goes over on his back. Every time.

It makes me think. We older fellers used to get issued with boots. In those days boots all had buckle sides on them so you could buckle them up. I think it must have been the late

'40s before R.M. Williams started making elastic-side boots, and then we all went to Williams. He made really good boots, R.M. Williams. One time I was out on Bedford Downs with my brother, old Joe Thomas. He's not an actual brother but his father was my mother's first husband, that's why I call him brother. We're catching this great big bull. I pulled him down all right, and I hung onto him and sung out to Joe, 'Come and give me a hand.' By this time I was stuffed, Joe was a bit slow, and the bull got up on me. Luckily there was an old bauhenia tree just about fifty yards away, and I ran for that tree. If I was to try and do it normally I would never have reached that branch, but I did reach it, and the horn of that bloody bull just caught me in the buckle of the boot and it ripped the boot right off me. I abused old Joe for being slow. He was a grown man and I was only about sixteen. I was one lucky man.

Another time at Whitewater we were mustering in the wet time, when there was plenty of green grass, and in that sort of feed the cattle get runny shit all down their tail. I was chasing a big old Friesian cow with horns about three foot wide. I tried to pull her, but I didn't lock the tail in my hand and she was too quick, plus when she spun around I slipped, and the horn sliced about four inches out of my side – lucky it didn't go into my guts.

I was terrible sore. I whacked the hot branding iron into the wound, just to give it a bit of a fright and keep it shut.

When that hapened to me Tom Quilty called me a useless bastard. 'Why the fuck didn't you put the fuckin' thing around your hand quick?' I didn't have a chance. If you made a mistake you didn't get a second chance. Everything you did had to be perfect.

When you were working out bush you weren't allowed to get sick. If you got sick you were only pretending, keeping away from work. I will say that one time I was sick with suspected appendix, and Quiltys took me into Halls Creek and they flew me to Derby to the hospital. The doctor was more interested in my citizenship than finding out what was wrong with me. I was crying with pain and he kept asking me, 'Have you got citizen's rights? If you haven't got citizen's rights you'll have to go to the Native Hospital.' In those days some people got a little book with a photo in it, like a driving licence, to say they had citizen's rights, but I never did. They sent me to the Native Hospital but they did not find what was wrong with me, so they sent me back to Springvale.

●

In 1944 Western Australia passed the Native Citizenship Rights Act, which granted conditional citizenship for Aboriginal people in that state. Anyone applying for citizenship had to give evidence that they had kept apart from tribal association for two years, had adopted the habits of civilised life, and were not suffering from leprosy, syphilis, granuloma or yaws. Aboriginal people nicknamed the licence the 'dog tag'. Charlie did not apply for citizenship rights.

**Charlie:**  Mustering used to last for about eight months of the year in the Kimberley, until the wet season. After the mustering we used to go back to the station and old Tom would give us the Willy jeep or some vehicle, to go over town for a bit of a break, maybe three or four days. After that we used to come back to Springvale and do repairs ready for the next season.

At the end of the mustering season we always used to grease our saddles and gear. Old Tom Quilty used to do most of the saddlery repairs himself. Most of the saddles we used in the stockcamps, packsaddles and bridles, were made by Yuill and Syd Hill in those early days. Some of the old fellers would make their own stuff. They'd buy their leather and they'd make things like reins, surcingles and stirrup leathers. A lot of them used to make their own saddles too. Doris Fletcher's husband, old

Charlie, was a great saddler. He used to make saddles by the hundreds at Moola Bulla. He used to make all sorts of gear, actually. Paddy McGinty used to be a good saddle maker. You could show him anything and he'd make it for you. He was taught by old Charlie Fletcher. He was a smart man, old Charlie.

Reins and bridles were just plain leather, and we used mainly the old snaffle bit with a join in the middle and a bar with a ring where you hook your reins.

A breastplate was an added thing on your saddle, if you were lucky to have one. It used to come down over the shoulders to a fork in the brisket, and there was a circle on it that went around the girth. I got mine from a feller called Archie Sturt from Moola Bulla, and it was a really well-made, good-looking thing too. It was all studded to make it look a bit flash. Tom used to always have a go at me about that. He didn't like it if you had a breastplate and yet he used to use one on his own horse. We always used a crupper under the tail for safety.

We used to make the halters ourselves out of greenhide and home-made rope. We made hobbles out of greenhide too. They were pretty hard and the horses used to get all sore, 'specially the colts when we used to first hobble them. The greenhide leather of the hobbles was hard at first, but we always made them as soft as possible and after a while they used to get real soft. We used to grease all the gear with a mixture of fat and kerosene, a four-gallon drum of fat boiled down with half a gallon of kero in to soften it up. The kerosene would help it to penetrate into the leather.

Besides the saddlery we used to do the repairs to the yards and all that sort of thing. In the wet we used to go and cut rails and yard posts and make new yards and return yards. There was always plenty of work, plenty of work.

At the beginning of the rainy season we used to go poddy-dodging with Tom Quilty and Basil Quilty. Tom would only take about two old blokes with him, usually my old uncle,

Yunguntji, and maybe one other bloke. But mainly it was just all us kids: myself, my brother Gilbo McAdam, Rusty Peters, Rammel, Russia, and Finnigan Quilty. We used to go poddy-dodging with Tom Quilty during the wet, around Moola Bulla mainly.

It used to rain, hail and storm. In that country, in the Kimberley, it really rains there. In bad weather we'd get bogged up to our knees sometimes. The rivers would be running, the creeks running, and when we used to get up in the morning everything would be wet, even our flour and tea and sugar. There was no such thing as Drizabones or oilskins up there. In winter when it was cold you might be lucky to have a jumper, or an old leather coat. In summer when it rained we used to just go and get the horses, and keep mustering.

We didn't know we were poddy-dodging at first. We though it was just part of mustering. Mustering – it wasn't mustering. It was cattle stealing. We used to end up with about four or five hundred head of cattle and we'd draft 'em out, all the big cleanskin weaners, big calves, even some bulls and cows, and take 'em back to Springvale, following the creeks so the water would cover our tracks and they wouldn't be able to track us. All this would take about three to four weeks. We'd take 'em back to Springvale, brand them up, then put them in a paddock for a month or two until they got used to the place.

One year I remember we went to Lansdowne Station, which Rod Quilty was managing by then. It was mainly the same kids I just mentioned, and we had a feller called Charlie Yeeda with us. He was a little bit older than myself, I think about four or five years older. We loaded up the packhorses and off we went to Lansdowne. When we got there we mustered the Lansdowne horse paddock and then set out for Fossil Downs. It was in the wet season of course. The packhorses were struggling to go across the rivers and creeks in that soft mud, because they were loaded down with all our swags and heavy packs.

We were poddy-dodging out around Fossil Downs for about two weeks and we had heaps and heaps of cattle, at least 2000 head. They were mainly Shorthorns, which were the cattle of the day in those days. There was no such thing as Brahmans up there until the middle '50s. We were drafting all the cleanskins, steers that were big enough to separate from their mother, big heifers, big mickys, lots of big micky bulls and mobs of cleanskin cows. Fossil Downs cattle never had an earmark. All they had was a brand, and old Tom was in his glory. The Quilty brand used to be TQ2.

When we got a mob of cattle together we used to have a good look for brands, and if you couldn't see the brand we'd draft them off. We even drafted off big bullocks if you couldn't see the brand. If I can remember rightly we ended up with about 1500 head of cleanskins and drove them back to Lansdowne.

Next morning early we mustered up the bronco horses. We branded about half the cattle that first day, and the next day we just started branding again when Rod Quilty and Charlie Yeeda had a bit of an argument. Rod reckoned we were bludging and Charlie, who was the overseer, stuck up for us. Rod walked back to the station homestead and picked up his revolver. We saw him coming back. About a hundred yards away from the yards he took the gunbelt off his hip and threw it under a little kungka berry bush.

I said to Charlie Yeeda, 'Hey Charlie, look where Quilty chucked his revolver under that little kungka berry bush there.'

'Oh, that's what he's up to, is he?'

I said, 'Looks like it. He might put a bullet through us, eh?'

When Rod Quilty jumped into the yards Charlie walked up to him and he said, 'What are you trying to prove, Rod?'

Rod said, 'What do you mean?'

'What's the idea of going to get the revolver over at the house and then chucking it behind the bush there?' said

Charlie. 'You think we didn't see you? You that much of a coward?' They had a big argument. Charlie went over to this bush and sure enough there was a revolver there in a pouch, and he got the revolver and smashed it up with the axe.

That night Charlie wasn't too sure whether to sleep or not, because he was afraid that Rod Quilty might come along and do him in. He shifted his swag further down the creek and hid away.

It took us all next day to walk the horses from Lansdowne to Bedford Downs after we packed all our gear up, mustered all our horses, and packed up the packhorses. We camped there at Bedford Downs that night, and the next day early, back we went with the horses to Springvale. At Springvale we told Tom Quilty all about what happened. He said nothing. He more or less backed his son up, and that was that.

Next day we took the shoes off our horses and let the horses out for a spell, to start again another season next year.

I often say to myself I wish they had helicopters in those days because Quiltys would have been spotted and caught and we would never have gone through all that rubbish. Old Tom Quilty, he's dead and gone now. I suppose it was all part of life.

One year we were attending the muster on Moola Bulla. Tending the muster means that we used to go to Moola Bulla and pick up all the Springvale cattle that had strayed there and bring them back to the station. That was a regular thing every year. Round the corner from where that Moon Dreaming is – the young moon in the creek bed – there's a place called Bullock Hole. That's part of Moola Bulla country, and that's where we'd attend the muster from Moola Bulla.

One of the stockmen on Moola Bulla was a feller called William Williams. This William Williams was sent away from Beagle Bay to Moola Bulla for a punishment. I don't know what Williams did at Beagle Bay, but he was sent to Moola Bulla. He was one of the few blokes that Alf George was scared of on Moola Bulla. I remember one time when I was a kid there, a feller called Tex Fuller and some other blokes had William Williams tied up to a post flogging him with a greenhide rope.

Anyway, now Tex Fuller was managing another place, I think it was Alice Downs, and we'd all come to Bullock Hole from the surrounding stations to attend the Moola Bulla muster. That's where this William Williams run into Tex Fuller. Tex said to him, 'How're you going mate?' and went to shake hands with him.

William Williams said to Tex, 'Remember that time at Moola Bulla when you tied me up on the saddle shed post?'

Tex said, 'Ah, come on, forget about it.'

William Williams said, 'Mate, I haven't forgotten yet. Come on, finish it off.' He gave that whitefeller the biggest thumping you've ever seen, and Tex couldn't open his eye for days after. Basil Quilty was going to jump in, but the other mob said, 'If you jump in you're only going to be in the same situation and you'll get smashed up too.' So Basil Quilty left us there and he went back to the station. He was too frightened.

Another year when Tom Quilty sent me and two other lads tending the muster on Moola Bulla, we left early in the morning. I was riding a grey mare and she was pretty fresh. Round about a mile or so from the station this mare started to buck. She bucked and bucked and she threw me. Then she galloped away, went through a fence and cut all her chest.

I caught her again but we had to go back into the station yards instead of continuing on to Moola Bulla. Tom Quilty asked, 'What's the matter?'

'Well, that mare threw me.'

'Where's the mare?'

'She's there, look, she's got a big cut in her chest.'

'You useless black bastard,' he said. 'Why didn't you hang onto her and stop her from bucking?' Of course I did my best to hang onto her. You can't stop a horse when she's frightened and bucking like that mare.

'Next time you do that, I'm gonna flog the daylights out of you,' Tom said.

Just about every night at Springvale before I'd go to sleep I'd always wonder to myself, There must be a better place to work. There must be a better boss to work for. This went on for two or three years until one year I decided to leave.

# The Long Paddock

**Charlie McAdam:** WE WERE BULLOCK mustering on Springvale, and when we eventually got up to the other end we had about 500 head of bullocks that we delivered to the feller who used to do most of the Springvale droving to Wyndham meatworks. He was an old half-Afghan feller called Darkie Green. That night before the delivery I said to Darkie, 'Any chance of a job, Darkie?'

He said, 'Yeah, if you want a job. I haven't got a spare saddle, but I've got a bridle.'

'Oh,' I said, 'it doesn't matter Darkie, I just want to get away from this place.'

He said, 'Yeah, no worries, you can come with me. I'm going to take delivery of the bullocks tomorrow afternoon.'

Basil Quilty was head stockman by then, so in the morning when we woke up I said to him, 'Basil, I'm leaving.' This is right out in the never-never and I had nothing, just a swag and a couple of shirts and trousers.

He said, 'What the bloody hell do you want to leave for?'

'Because I don't like working on Springvale,' I said. 'It's too hard for me, and I want to go and travel and have a look at the country.'

By this time he was standing over my swag, wanting to fight me.

I got up and said, 'Yeah, I'll fight you – any time.' I think he was a bit frightened because my old uncle Yunguntji and all my relatives on my mother's side were there, and he backed off. He said, 'Righto, piss off. Away you go.'

He went over to Darkie Green and he said to Darkie, 'What the hell are you doin', givin' Charlie a job?'

Darkie said, 'Well, he asked me last night for a job and I'm a bit short, I could do with another man.'

And Basil said, 'This is the last mob of cattle you'll ever take from Springvale, Darkie.'

'Okay,' said Darkie. 'Fair enough. There's other stations beside Springvale, mate.'

In the end I went with Darkie Green. It used to take from three to four weeks to drive a mob of bullocks from the place on Springvale where we took delivery to Wyndham meatworks. The first week on the road we were watering the mob of cattle at one of the creeks there. I was riding along a high part of the bank when it gave way underneath me, and me and the horse went tumbling down, over and over. I broke my arm at the elbow, and boy, wasn't I in pain. Had no medicine, had nothing actually.

Luckily there was a feller with us called Joe Atkinson. I knew Joe from years before when he was breaking in horses on Springvale for Jimmy McAdam. He was an Australian bronc riding champion known throughout the Australian rodeo circuit. He taught me a lot about horses on that droving trip, and he fixed my arm. He got a bark off a tree and used an old blanket to wrap round my arm on the bark as a sling. That didn't relieve it very much but I believe it kept it stable. The horse that

I was riding was an old horse, a very quiet horse, and he was that slow in walking, but with this broken arm he still wasn't slow enough. Every jar from the hoof I could feel. I was in agony for three weeks.

The stock route from Bedford used to cut straight north out through Bedford Downs and come out on the main road at Card Creek, about three days' droving from Wyndham. The cattle were tired and lame after travelling through the stony country. About twenty-five miles from Wyndham is the jump-up where the road goes up through a cutting over the hill, with only enough room for cattle to go through one at a time alongside the road. We had to string the cattle out to go through the jump-up and hope that a truck wouldn't go through. If a truck did go through, the cattle would stop or turn back and it would be hard to get them going again.

Just before the jump-up is a permanent water hole called Crocodile Hole, and every drover used to camp there so the cattle could rest before going through the jump-up. On one side of the creek the bank is flat and grassy, an easy place to water cattle. There was always bream, catfish, freshwater crocodile in that pool. We camped under the big boab tree there, it's still standing today, and while we were there we met another drover feller called Billy Laurie. He was heading back to a place called Texas with an empty plant, just the stockhorses and packhorses, after he'd finished delivering his cattle. Billy Laurie knew Darkie Green. Actually he was living with Darkie's ex-wife, Amy Laurie, who used to be a top woman drover in her day. We had dinner there with him. Darkie never drank, but this Billy Laurie feller had a couple of bottles of rum with him and after a few drinks he was charged up and he started to get a bit nasty with Darkie.

'Yeah, Darkie,' he reckoned, 'I'm looking after three of your kids and you ought to be givin' me money to support them.' In the end they started fighting. Darkie ended up giving him a hiding. Darkie jumped on his horse and came round to where we had the cattle and away we went in a hurry to get out of there, but this Billy Laurie feller jumped on his horse with a great butcher's knife and he chased Darkie. He caught up to Darkie and almost sliced his arm off at the shoulder. It was very lucky for Darkie that a truck came through. He managed to get a lift into Wyndham to the hospital and left Joe Atkinson in charge of the mob.

At the time that those two blokes were fighting we missed a few head of cattle because we were panicking in our hurry to get out of there. It took us another two days to get to Wyndham, and when we delivered the cattle I think we were a hundred short.

We went to see Darkie in hospital. The first thing he said was, 'What happened? You blokes missed a hundred head of cattle.'

We said, 'Yeah.'

'Why?'

'Well,' I said, 'I think we might have lost 'em when you and Bill Laurie was fighting at Crocodile Hole.'

'Oh shit, yeah, okay then.'

Anyway, Tom Quilty wrote a letter to Darkie Green at Wyndham. It said that he'd heard what happened to Darkie, and in the letter he said that he supposed it was Charlie McAdam's fault because he was a typical blackfeller, no sense of responsibility and wouldn't care how many cattle were lost. So I got the blame from old Tom, as if I was the boss drover there or second in charge or something like that, when actually I was the lad that had no responsibility at the time.

After we delivered the cattle we made a camp at Six Mile, right near the old hotel there that was once owned by my dad. While we were there I got very friendly with a white girl called Shirley. I actually gave her a ring. I wasn't allowed to go to parties because I was a blackfeller, so we used to sit outside on

Jimmy McAdam with
Faye and Elliot, at
Elliott, 1950s

Mick Quilty, a visiting pastor's son, Finnigan Quilty, and Gilbert McAdam
Senior, at Springvale around 1949

Charlie on horseback at Lake Nash, early 1960s

Some of Charlie's fellow stockmen at Lake Nash, early 1960s; Frank Byrne is on the left

Jack Tjugarai outside Old Halls Creek police station, 1993, holding a loop of the chain that was used to restrain Aboriginal prisoners

The saddle shed on Bedford Downs where the electrocutions took place

Russia Clifton, Gilbert
McAdam Senior and
Rammel Peters, at
Springvale, 1950s

The river near Springvale homestead where Ngamarranye the snake lies

Gilbert McAdam Senior and Evelyn on their wedding day at Halls
Creek, 1969

Charlie and Yunguntji on Bedford Downs, 1993

The McAdam children in Alice Springs, 1984. Back row: Greg, Ian; middle row: Margaret, Pamela, Michelle, Elizabeth; front row: Gilbert, Adrian (Photo courtesy of Steve Strike)

Adrian and Val McAdam at Traeger Park, late 1980s

Charlie with Rudolf
Newman in Broome,
1993

Tjulaman with granddaughter Jenice
at Halls Creek, 1994

Debbie McAdam at the
Halls Creek Rodeo, 1993

Greg McAdam captaining the South Alice Springs Football Club in their first premiership, 1984. Greg won the Everingham Medal for the best player in the grand final

The best of rivals – Adrian and Gilbert McAdam, 1993 (Photo courtesy of Mirror Australian Telegraph Publications)

the verandah and she'd shout me a cool drink or I'd shout her a cool drink of lemonade or something like that. Aboriginal people weren't allowed to drink grog in those days and I didn't drink until I was well into my thirties.

One night I was with Shirley sitting outside on the verandah and three white blokes came by. They said to Shirley, 'Who's your black boyfriend here?'

She said, 'That's Charlie, he's from Springvale Station.'

'Doesn't matter who he is but he's a nigger. How come you got mixed up with a nigger like that?'

I jumped up and I was going to have a go. I wasn't afraid. Shirley grabbed hold of me and said, 'Don't do that Charlie. I'll see the manager.'

Still I wanted to have a go at them. I knew there was three of them and I didn't have a chance against three, but I wanted to have a go for the way they called me a nigger. Shirley ran off and told the manager there, a feller called Jeff, who came out and asked her the same question. He said, 'What are you doing with Charlie here?'

She said, 'He's a good friend of mine and these fellers came along and asked me what I was doing with a nigger.' I don't know what he said to the blokes after that, but they all went back into the bar and nothing happened.

It was one of those things that when blokes saw a blackfeller with a white woman in those days it was a mortal sin, something terrible. They reckoned if a white girl went with a blackfeller she was lower than the lowest. Shirley and I didn't take much notice of that because we were very good friends at the time.

Before I go any further, I'm going to go back to Springvale.

When I was on Springvale working there for those few years I used to be told by Tom Quilty, Basil Quilty, all the white people there, 'You're not a bloody blackfeller, you're a yellerfeller, you're a white man, you don't want to mix with those blackfellers.' They always tried to drum it into me that I wasn't a blackfeller. Even my mother was poisoned. She said to me in lingo, 'You not blackfeller. You ngilaping [half-caste]. You don't want to mix up with black women or anything like that.' Said this when I came back to Springvale. She always worked for white people all her life and I suppose my father told her that, or the Quiltys, she probably got it from the white man's influence. I tried not to take much notice but actually at one stage I started to believe them because of my colour.

One day old Tom Quilty told Basil and me to go out and shoot all the camp dogs, because there were too many of them. My grandparents were still camped there on the little rocky knob up behind the homestead. Basil and I shot their dogs, too, along with the rest.

My grandfather said to me, in Kija, 'We brought you up. We looked after you all those years and now you shoot our dogs. Do you think you're katiya?'

I'll always remember that.

It didn't matter where I went. When I was sent to Moola Bulla, to Beagle Bay, or later when I went to the Centre mustering, even in Alice Springs, people used to say the same thing. 'What do you want to mix with those blackfellers for? You're not a bloody blackfeller, you're a half-caste, you should be like a white man and forget all about those blacks.'

They tried to drum it into my brains, and they almost did because you know everywhere where I went I'd hear, 'You're not a blackfeller, you're a half-caste, you're like a white man.' They almost convinced me that I wasn't Aboriginal. It took me a long time to work that out. In the end I thought back to my old mother and my family and I knew who I was.

Whitefellers used to say these things to us, and yet they used to go and have sex with Aboriginal women. Almost every day they used to go down to the camp and bully the poor old fellers, and get their daughters or maybe their young wives. The men couldn't do anything about it because they'd be frightened they'd be shot. Thank God those days are gone by.

Basil Quilty was always saying that we weren't blackfellers, we were yellerfellers, that we should live like white men, all that sort of thing, and yet he had five children with my cousin Lou Lou. He was managing Bedford Downs then. When the eldest kid was about ten, Basil married a white woman who was the governess on Inverway Station. Lou Lou eventually moved to Springvale.

When Welfare asked her if she wanted the kids to have the Quilty surname, Lou Lou refused. 'No, they'll be right,' she said. After a while she married again, to Martin Trankilino, who was a very smart feller from Beagle Bay.

Those were the things that were happening in those days. In the Kimberley, and even in the Northern Territory, they had three types of people – white people; yellerfellers, half-caste, or whatever you like to call them; and blackfellers. Even today around Halls Creek they don't class half-caste people as blackfellers. And yet half-caste people, they all identify themselves as Aboriginals. I do, and a lot of people back home do. I find it different in the southern states, now, because if you are a part-Aboriginal person you are classed as an Aboriginal. But back in the Kimberley and the Territory, it's still happening today: if you are half-caste you cop it from both sides. That's life, I suppose. But you come over to Melbourne and you're a blackfeller. Actually I was talking to the daughter of an old friend of mine in Melbourne not long ago, young Bernadette Fagan.

She said, 'Are you full-blood, Charlie?'

I said, 'No, look at my colour, I'm in between.'

Bernadette was a bit embarrassed. She said, 'Well, I don't know.'

I knew. I understood straight away. She'd never seen a blackfeller in her life. She give me a bit of a compliment. She said, 'Well, you're a very nice person anyway, Charlie.'

I said, 'Thank you, Bernadette.' I had to laugh.

Anyway, back to the droving days. A week or ten days after he got out of hospital Darkie Green bought a truck and we set off back to Halls Creek.

Darkie Green used to suffer with a bad back, very bad. Sometimes he'd stiffen up so he could hardly walk. He had been to see different doctors but no one had been able to help him. On the way back he said to me, 'I'm going to go see an old bloke, see if he can fix my back up.' When we got to Mabel Downs we made camp and went over to see the old feller, whose whitefeller name was Walter. He was a very gifted man, a well-respected doctor, and I suppose you could describe him as a magician.

When the old feller saw me, he said, 'Eh, you Yurudtji, from Springvale?'

'Yeah.' He gave me a big hug because he was related to my mother too.

When we were kids this old feller used to do some tricks for us with shells, all shaped like boomerangs. He used to dig a hole in the ground, only about three or four inches deep, and he'd put three shells in this hole and he'd put his finger over it. We kids would get a pannikin of water and pour it over the top of his hands, and he'd take his hand away from the hole and there'd be no shells there. We would be amazed, we'd be looking around, and he'd say, 'Oh, they're there somewhere. I know where they are, I'll show you in a minute.' We'd look around but we couldn't see the shells.

Usually there was a tree about three to four yards from where he was sitting, a special type of corkwood with pretty soft wood. He'd say, 'You look on the tree there, look. Them shells are there.' And we used to have a look at this tree and sure enough those shells would be sticking out of this tree. I just don't know what he used to do, but if he did flick them over when no one was looking he must have been a good shot to stick those shells into that tree. Another thing he used to do was throw just one little shell in the same hole and put his hand over it, and then he'd tell us to get a billy can of water or a bucket of water and pour it over his hand, and next thing there'd be maybe half a dozen shells in there. I just couldn't believe what he used to do with those shells.

There's another story about this old bloke. Years ago, these doctors used to come around to inspect Aboriginal people. They used to strip us kids off, feel us here, feel us there. They did the same to the grown-up people. I was there one time when one of these doctors came around to this old feller Walter. The doctor examined him. There was nothing wrong with the old feller.

Walter said to the doctor, 'Anything wrong with me?'

Doctor said, 'No, you're all right.'

Old feller put his hand on the left-hand side of his chest. I don't know what he did, but it looked as though he got something out of his chest, and when he showed it to the doctor, it looked like it was a black rock or something like that and the doctor couldn't believe it. Then he said to the doctor, 'Is there something wrong with you?'

The doctor said, 'No, nothing wrong with me.'

Walter said, 'Give me your finger, Doctor, something wrong with you.' He took hold of the doctor's finger and blood started to squirt out of the point of the finger. That was amazing. That white doctor just could not believe what was going on.

Then old Walter said to him, 'Doctor, you've got something in your ear.' The doctor sort of felt his ear and he said, 'No, I've got nothing there.' This old feller put his hand over the doctor's ear and pulled something else out. The white doctor could not believe that the other old bloke was also a doctor. Aboriginal doctors used to be classed as witch doctors, but to me, and to every Aboriginal person in the Kimberley, Walter was well respected. He was classed as a top doctor as far as every Aboriginal was concerned.

At Mabel Downs, Darkie went to see him and asked the old feller if he could come over and fix his back, and he said, 'Yeah, I'll come over there later on.'

That evening Darkie laid on his swag with his aching back, and the old feller got over the top of his back and started rubbing it. What amazed me was that he told Darkie Green almost all his movements in the last twelve months. He said to Darkie, 'Oh, you been in so-and-so country and you've been to this place and that place,' naming the places. Darkie could not believe it because all those places that he mentioned, that's where Darkie had been. Anyway, Walter was rubbing his back, backwards and forwards, backwards and forwards, with his hand. Then he stuck his mouth over his spine, right down the bottom of his back, and he started sucking, and at the same time he had one hand on the upper part of his back and the other on the lower part of his back towards his bottom there. As he was sucking he was spitting out what looked like great big hunks of dried blood. I don't know what the hell they were. White man always tells you that it's all bullshit, the blackfeller bites his tongue and makes it bleed, making out he's sucking the blood out of you, but this didn't look like blood from his tongue, it was all in big hunks. He kept rubbing and rubbing, he kept sucking and spitting it out, and he eventually couldn't suck any more out of him. In an hour Darkie Green was as good as gold. He jumped up, walked around, he couldn't feel a thing in his back.

About three years ago I ran into Darkie Green in Kununurra, and I said to him, 'Hey Darkie, remember that time when that old feller fixed your back up? Did you ever have any trouble with that back since?' And he said, 'Never ever had any trouble with that back, that old feller fixed it right up for me.' Isn't that amazing? I saw him fix Darkie's back up and

Darkie told me that he'd been to a few doctors and they couldn't do anything for him, and this Aboriginal feller fixed him up. That's one of the amazing things that Aboriginal people can do. He was a gifted man, old Walter.

When Darkie and I got back to Halls Creek we didn't have a job, but we weren't short of a quid – we had a few pound, used to be pounds in those days. A feller called David Skeen asked me if I wanted a job, and I said, 'Yeah, what doin'?' And he said, 'Droving to the Territory.' I said, 'Oh, beauty, yeah, no worries!'

We packed our gear and mustered up a few horses on Sophie Downs Station. From Sophie Downs we had to go through Flora Valley Station, to a place called Wallamunga Waterhole on Birrindudu Station in the Territory. That's where we took delivery of 1500 head of cows and calves. There were three or four of us ringers driving the cattle, a cook, and another feller drivin' the horses. That was a normal droving team – boss drover, three or four ringers, cook and horse tailer.

It was very hot weather and the country was pretty dry. There wasn't very much rain that year. Things went really good, taking these cows and calves along the track. We only were doing about six miles a day because the cows and the calves were very weak. I think that trip ended up taking us about four months in all.

●

This trip, with 1500 head of Birrindudu cows and calves, followed the Murranji Track, notorious for being the most difficult stock route in terms of terrain and scarcity of water. The Murranji took its name from a desert frog capable of living underground without water for long periods. Crossing the Murranji was a badge of honour in a drover's cap, and the list of names in the Stockmen's Hall of Fame of those who have done so comprises mainly white men – the boss drovers.

Throughout Australia all movement of cattle until the mid 1950s was by overlanding cattle along a network of stock routes, which are still used today in times of drought in certain areas. Major routes followed the tracks of the first cattle drives, and the movement of increasing numbers of cattle and sheep created a maze of stock routes more numerous than roads in the eastern states. The land occupied by the routes is government owned, and the routes themselves are managed by regional or state authorities. Movement along the routes is subject to regulation and payment of fees, and drovers need to obtain permission to take stock through any stations which lie on the routes.

When droving cattle through arid country there was always the danger that a mob of thirsty cattle smelling water would rush a waterhole and become hopelessly bogged in the mud. A thousand-head rush of stampeding cattle was unstoppable. Drovers had to call on all their skills to move the mob along gently, keeping them upwind from the scent of water, sometimes walking at night to minimise dehydration, easing the mob towards its destination.

There were other problems, apart from the terrain, for drovers.

**Charlie:**  When we got to Top Springs the trouble started. There was a little bit of a roadside hotel there, owned by a Mrs Hawke. David Skeen the boss drover, a feller called Jerry Waterhouse, Dick Darcy and Harry Bray got on the rum. They bought a couple of cases of rum and they put them in an old T-model Ford. Any rate, they were drunk from Top Springs right to Elliott. All the way along from Top Springs to Newcastle Waters, the three that took these cattle were the three blackfellers: myself, a feller called Otto Sampi, and Sandy Rivers. Otto Sampi was a full-blood feller, from Beagle Bay actually. We were the only ones not drinking. We three blokes and one old blue dog took the cattle right through to Elliot. It was hard work watching those cattle with the other blokes drunk all the time.

The old blue dog there, we called him Bluey, was a big help to us. In the end, that dog knew as soon as a cow walked away from the mob at night and he'd run around and bring it back to the mob. He ended up being a very good dog. We travelled along, just taking it as it comes, and watering the cattle every second day. By the time we got near Newcastle Waters those cattle were perishing for water. As soon as they smelt the water they started to rush.

Otto Sampi and Sandy Rivers and I tried to hold these cattle but we just could not hold them. They were galloping both sides all round us. To make matters worse, our poor old horses were very weak and we couldn't do very much with them. The manager of Newcastle Waters Station came along and said, 'Bloody hell, what's going on? You've got all these cattle mixing up with my cattle.' He went on and on. In the end I just said to him, 'Look, our boss drover's back there, drunk as a skunk. All his mates are drunk, there's just three of us and we just can't hold 'em.'

He realised what had really happened after I had a talk to him, and he was very sympathetic towards us. Luckily the cattle that we had didn't mix up with his cattle. We watered the cattle there and kept going to Elliott. The towns of Newcastle Waters and Elliott were just little places with a store and a pub where the drovers used to stop over.

While I was at Elliott I received a message from my father. He was living there at the time. After he sold Springvale to Tom Quilty in '48 he bought a store and a grog shop at Newcastle Waters. He sold that to a feller called Jack Siden and then he went into partnership with Max Schobers in Elliott. He told David Skeen, 'You tell Charlie I want to see him.' I hadn't seen my father since I was taken to Moola Bulla as a little kid, but I decided I'd call in to see him on the way back.

After Elliott we hit the Barkly stock route. I did a few droving trips across the Barkly in my time. We always had to carry water there, in water bags and quart pots. We had canvas water bags, but the water bag never lasted long carrying it on the horse because the top gets bumped off going along. They didn't have screw-tops in those days, just a leather roll pushed into the neck of the bottle. You had a neck bag and a shoulder bag, and you could fill them both full of water, but in half an hour you would only have half a bag of water left.

On the Barkly Tableland you don't see wood for miles. You could go maybe one full day without seeing wood, then the next day you might camp beside a gully with a few trees in it. Sometimes we'd load up the packhorse with wood because the next day we would be riding out in open country again.

When there was no wood we used to light dried-up cow dung to try and boil the billy. Actually we'd use our quart pots, because they're smaller than the billy and it's easier to get them to boil. Sometimes it was hard work to make half a pot of tea.

On that particular trip we didn't have much time for cooking. When we killed a killer we boiled it up, grabbed a bit and kept going. We would be riding along with the cooked up rib-bones sticking out of our saddlebags. It was pretty rough.

We delivered those cattle to a place called Helen Springs, about 150 short because of ironwood poisoning along the Murranji Track. The cattle ate the bark off the trees and the ironwood there is poisonous. But we could have lost the lot if they'd rushed the waterholes along the track.

After we delivered the cattle, we stayed there for a couple of days and then went back to Elliott. I found my father was married to a woman called Dorcas Wesley and he had two kids from her. They're my brother and sister, Elliot McAdam and

Faye McAdam. I don't know whether he was glad to see me or not, but he shook hands with me and I stayed there with him for a while, on account of he was my dad.

●

When Jimmy McAdam met Dorcas Wesley, she had five children from a previous marriage, Helen, Heather, Kenny, Billy and Dorothy, whom Jimmy raised along with Faye and Elliot. 'He could be a tough old feller,' recalls Heather. 'But he loved our mother, and he really loved those two little kids, Faye and Elliot.'

Elliot McAdam's memories of his father are of a kindly old man who drove him to school every day. His first impression of his older brother Charlie was of a tall, wiry figure, fit and athletic.

At the time, Jimmy McAdam was in partnership with Max Schobers in the Elliott store. The store sold a variety of goods and had a two-gallon licence, which meant that liquor could only be sold over the counter in quantities of two gallons or more. The preferred drink of drovers at the time was rum topped up with a dash of port. As a child Elliot recalled that neither his mother, who was a strong Christian woman, nor his father drank, but Jimmy McAdam knew all the drovers, who would camp out of town and congregate at the store. McAdam organised football and cricket matches, and there were some wild parties.

In his late sixties Jimmy McAdam was still a practical joker. One morning he surveyed the ringers sleeping soundly on iron beds outside the store after a drinking session the night before. He tied each bed-frame in turn to his truck and towed them out onto the flat, leaving the ringers to wonder how they got there when they awoke.

Among the regular visitors to Elliott were Mick Coomb, Jimmy McAdam's lifelong friend, and his wife Olive from Halls Creek, who passed through with mobs of cattle en route to Dajarra. Elliot remembers that his first ride, and fall, from a horse was from the pommel of Olive's saddle when her mount shied.

When Mick married Olive after the war, it was so unusual for a white man to marry an Aboriginal woman that it made headlines.

**Mick Coomb:**   When we come out of the army, none of us were sound. Well, we weren't sound or we wouldn't have got into it. I didn't like authority, I'd had too much of it. Like a kid with watermelon – you stuff 'em up with too much and then they won't eat it. I was in Wyndham once with Olive – she was a very pretty girl, Olive – I was having a drink in the pub, and the Native Affairs officer, who was also the local policeman, was having a go at me, tellin' me I'd have to get a permit to employ a native. So I give him a bit of his pedigree, and said, 'Listen, Andrews, stop kickin' up a fuss. I'll go and bring the girl over to the police station and I'll marry her.' And I did.

I still do believe there should be a monument in every park in every country town to the native girls of this country, right next to the Anzac memorial. My wife Olive used to ride the boss's own camp horse at Lissadell, cutting out cattle. One time she took a mob of 1500 Beetaloo bullocks from Number Seven Dip to Yelvertoff, just this side of Mt Isa. Two boys and I did the cooking and horse-tailing because I couldn't get anyone else to cook, and she handled those cattle all the way, and nothing's ever said about her. They did a great job, those women, and without them I don't think the country would have been settled.

●

Charlie saw another side of his father at Elliott.

**Charlie:**   David Skeen paid Otto Sampi and I with a cheque. We went over to cash our cheque at the store, and after all that the cheque bounced. That's one thing I'll say about my old man, he helped me at that time. He went to see the police and I think the copper's name was Gordon Stock, from Newcastle Waters.

He said, 'Look, David Skeen owes these two boys money because this cheque bounced. Can we 'pound those horses, pack saddle, truck, everything?'

The copper said, 'Yes, go ahead, Jim, we'll 'pound the bastard until he makes his cheque come good.' The old man impounded them. Then he said to David Skeen, 'Okay they're not leaving, the plant and horses, or that truck – they're not leaving until Charlie and that Otto Sampi's cheque's all cleared.'

'You can't do that,' David Skeen said.

'Oh, yes I can.'

I think we waited a week, maybe two weeks, but the cheque was cleared and away they went. Otto Sampi and I stayed there with the old man, and if I can remember rightly the old man helped Otto Sampi to get a lift right back to Kununurra with a bloke who was going there to work. That was one good thing the old man did for Otto. I don't know what happened to Otto after that, but I haven't seen him since. I'd like to see him again so we could have a good old yarn about the trip that we had. That was the hardest trip I've been on and I've done a few droving trips in my time.

After Otto left I stayed there with the old man for a while at Elliott, carting some wood for him. He and Maxie Schobers had a truck and I carted a bit of wood for them. Back in those days there used to be only wood stoves.

We used to sit around at night yarning, and that was when the old man told me the stories about old Wason Byers. Byers used to manage stations in the Kimberley and I'd heard about him before.

My Dad told me that when Byers was managing Bradshaw's Run he was pinching cattle from Victoria River Downs next door.

Victoria River Downs' brand was just a bull's head, and the Bradshaw brand was the initials MTQ, so Byers was doing 'MT', and then 'Q' over the bull's head, trying to smudge that bull's head.

Anyway they caught him and he had to go to court. The old man reckoned he gave him money to help him out. Wason Byers had a lawyer called Jack Travis up from Adelaide. I think it was costing him something like £500 a day, that's why the old man gave away £1500. When they went to court they had all the Aboriginal ringers as witnesses, and Jack Travis cross-examined them.

Travis said, 'You know when you mustering cattle, you flog 'em with a whip, you make a mark on their back. Might have been a whip mark on that brand, eh?'

'Yeah, might be, might be whip mark, yeah.' Blackfeller always tries to agree with the white man. Yes is better than no.

'What about when you chase them cattle through that scrub and that, might be they scratch their rump, might make mark?'

'Yeah, might be, might be too.'

Old Wason, he never got involved in the work, he just supervised the Aboriginal people. So the Aboriginal stockmen were the ones actually cross-branding the cattle. In the end the old man reckoned the judge asked them, 'Who bin cross-branding those cattle?'

'Oh, me and all the boys bin branding those cattle.'

'Which way was Mr Wason?' [Where was Mr Wason?]

'Oh, he bin sit down in the camp. The boys bin do it.'

'Aah.'

Everyone laughed. That's how old Wason got out of it. When the policeman went to shake his hand after the court case Wason Byers refused to shake his hand. He said, 'I'd love to meet you in a bullwaddy scrub somewhere, I'd burn you alive.'

The Halls Creek mob have their own stories about Wason Byers. He was a man who got away with terrible things and nothing was ever done about it. People don't know what happened in those times. Jack Johnson is a sort of cousin of mine from Halls Creek. He was working on Flora Valley when Byers was manager.

**Jack Johnson:**   We knew old Wason Byers at Flora Valley. He used to strip the women naked and make them walk around. He used to flog the men and take their clothes off. One time he made the women take all their clothes off and sit up on top of the roof, on that sheet iron. It was 40 degrees temperature and he made them sit there all day, and he was chucking rocks at them to make them move around. He used to go out in the desert and try and track anyone who ran away from the station, and if he got 'im he would flog 'im there, put a chain around his neck and lead him back to the station and keep him tied up on the chain so he wouldn't do it again. Even the women. He was very cruel to them.

He used to go around with a .303 rifle on his saddle shooting all the people's dogs, and old Lou Brown, Jimmy Brown's father, he wanted to have a go at him. He had all boomerangs, but one boomerang's no good against a bullet. Jimmy Brown used to tell us, 'Wason Byers shot my father.'

We knew Wason Byers. We knew him too long.

When he was down at Coolibah Station there was one feller playing the didgeridoo.

'Who's been playing that didgeridoo all night?'

'Me.'

'By golly you can blow. You go and get that didgeridoo down the camp.'

That feller got the didgeridoo and then Wason Byers tied him up to a post. He made 'im blow that didgeridoo non-stop all day till sunset. Never give him a chance to have a spell, throw spit away or drink water – he made him blow from morning till dark. That feller's lips were swollen up and got stuck in the didgeridoo.

He was just as cruel to whitefellers. He pulled a gun on two fellers at Flora Valley, made them take off their trousers and sit on the hot fuel stove. He wasn't good to anyone, didn't matter if he was black or white. He always had to fight. Something wrong with him.

**Charlie:**   Years later, I met Wason Byers in Camooweal, one time when we were droving a mob of cattle from Eva Downs. He was a really old man then. He said, 'Oh, you're Jimmy McAdam's son!'

I said, 'Yeah.' And he said, 'How're you going? Old Jimmy was a good friend of mine. He helped me out a lot.'

One old feller, he was a funny old feller they used to call Lovely Charlie, a whitefeller, knew all about this Wason Byers. Lovely Charlie came along, drunk of course.

'Mr Wason, tough man of the nor'west,' he said. 'You're fucked now, aren't you.'

'Piss off you bastard,' said Wason Byers.

Lovely Charlie kept having a go at him, until Wason said to him, 'By the lovin' Jesus, Lovely,' he said to him, 'if ever I catch you in a bullwaddy scrub I'll burn you alive, you bastard.' Poor old Wason. That was his favourite saying. I believe he eventually died of cirrhosis of the liver. They reckon he was a terrible criminal man, especially with Aboriginal people.

# Man, Family Man

**Charlie McAdam:**    I WAS THERE at Elliott with my father for
maybe a month. After that I took off, travelling here and there
and everywhere. I did a few droving trips, all through the Territory and over to Dajarra. Dajarra was the biggest trucking
yards in the country then. It's just a ghost town now. Droving
wasn't continuous work, it was seasonal, during the dry.
During the wet the boss drovers would put you off. I used to end
up at Alice Springs or Mt Isa, and that was when I started
boxing and roughriding, to get a few quid.

Boxing was the sport Aboriginal people followed in those
days. When we were kids at Beagle Bay we'd hear about Dave
Sands or we'd read something in a newspaper about boxing, and
we used to wrap a towel or a shirt around our hands and we
used to box. The Sands brothers were six Aboriginal fellers
from around Kempsey in New South Wales. Dave Sands was
number two in the world at one stage. He was going to fight
Sugar Ray Robinson for the world title and Sugar Ray made a

statement to the paper, 'If I'm going to fight that guy I want big money for him.' But that fight never eventuated.

A lot of Aboriginal blokes couldn't get jobs and so they'd think, Oh well, I'll go boxing, I might be Australian champion or something. They followed in the footsteps of boxers like the Sands brothers, and Jack Hassen – he was one of the great fighters, from Cloncurry in Queensland. There were quite a few of them: Georgie Bracken from Palm Island, a great Aboriginal fighter; Ron Richards; Elliott Bennett, he could have been a world champion but usually it just got back down to being a blackfeller. They didn't have the opportunity. I think Lionel Rose was the first Aboriginal to get that opportunity to become a world champion.

For me it all started when a boxing troupe from Mt Isa came to Alice Springs. I wasn't trained but I liked boxing, and a feller called Joe Lewis who used to train in Alice Springs asked me and a few other ringers to go over there and spar there a couple of times in the off season. One day he said, 'There's a Mt Isa troupe coming up here to fight Alice Springs. Do you want to fight tonight?' I said, 'Yeah, no worries.' The bloke from Mt Isa came up and I knocked him out in the first round and that gave me encouragement. That was how I started.

My mates and I, we always fought under bodgie names. We didn't want our mob back home to know we were fighting. I used to fight as Joe West. When I first started boxing I won a few fights at Mt Isa, and I went to Townsville, won a few fights there, went to Sydney, won a couple of fights there. Then I went to Melbourne for about six weeks and had about three or four fights in that famous old stadium Festival Hall. I think I lost about four out of twenty fights. I was going all right, but we were getting ripped off all the time. White trainers, they knew Aboriginal people were good fighters and they'd see you coming a mile away and they'd rip you right off. You might fight ten rounds for about ten quid, something like that, and the trainer would take the rest. We were getting about £30 or £40 a week and we reckoned we were rich, but not one of the Aboriginal boxers ever had any money after he retired. Georgie Bracken might have ended up with a few bucks and a house, and I think Lionel might have bought a house and his mother living in it now, but it was just the same old story. I don't know whether it was only blackfellers getting ripped off, I think it used to happen to the young whitefellers too. Sometimes, if you put up a good fight, people would shower money into the ring, two-bob pieces, shillings, they'd just chuck it in the ring. There might have been £10 or £15 lying there, but you'd never see that money.

Boxing was a very popular sport in those days. There were boxing troupes travelling all over the country. I never fought in Jimmy Sharman's tent, although I knew some boxers from there. I fought in a couple of tents, one at Mt Isa and one in Alice Springs, but once you fight in a tent it's all a put-up job. I remember one day at Dajarra, Larry Dalhunty turned up with his travelling boxing tent. He had Alfie Clay, an ex-British champion, fighting for him, but Alfie was getting old. There was a feller there called Billy Dempsey, from Dajarra, a local lad. He was a brawler himself. Larry Dalhunty turned up with his boxing troupe, and the first night he's outside the tent spruiking.

'I've got a former British champion. Is anybody going to knock him out?'

There used to be three two-minute rounds, and if anybody knocked Alfie out he got £50. Anyway this Billy Dempsey jumped into the ring with him, and Alfie just lay down. Next night Dalhunty's up there spruiking again.

'Anybody . . . Where's that feller that knocked Alfie out the other day? Does he want to double the bet?'

The crowd yelled out, 'Yeah he's here!'

'Anybody want to back him? Alfie's going to have another go at him!'

Out comes all the money – £10 here, £20 there – all over the place. And poor old Billy was out cold in the first round.

Trainers used to praise me up. 'You're good and you're going to go a long way.' In 1955, when I went into the Northern Territory, the Olympics were coming up in Melbourne and trainers were telling me all sorts of stories, but in the end I thought, This is a mug's game. So I chucked it away.

I used to think about where I was going to end up, and how I would end up. I was frightened of brain damage, too. I never ever fought outside the ring. I always tried to avoid it because I've got that horrible temper. That's one thing I had to learn to control when I was boxing. I never looked for a fight outside the ring.

I don't like to talk about it. Some of my mates in Alice Springs ask me if I went boxing and I say, 'Nuh, bullshit.' Frank Byrne and I have been mates since we were kids, and even Frank only found out about it from someone else. A feller I used to spar with was talking to Frank at a funeral in Darwin.

Frank said to me, 'I didn't know you went boxing, Bruz! Why didn't you tell me?'

I said, 'No, I didn't want to skite about it.'

The other feller said, 'Yeah, he wasn't bad this feller, he knocked a few out when he went to Melbourne and Sydney, but the bastard wouldn't stay on.' It was a mug's game, that's why I left.

I hate fighting, and yet I followed it in my young days. I never ever taught my kids how to box either, because I didn't want them to be fighters. They might have been good at that. They're good at everything else.

I started roughriding at the rodeos about the same time, when I was droving in Queensland with Clarrie Pankhurst. We did a couple of trips from Marion Downs to Winton, and then from Camooweal to Winton. If there was no work we hopped in a car – if we had a car – or jumped on a bus and travelled to where the rodeo was on. I rode in Camooweal, Mt Isa, Cloncurry, Winton, Meribah, and back through the same places again. I rode horses and bulls – saddle bronco, bareback, and the bull ride. There used to be some top riders riding at that time: Brian Young, the Country and Western singer now, and his brother Bonny Dunkham, Wally Woods, Vic Gough. I won a few and lost a few, got thrown and got busted up.

Sometimes you might win. Prize money ranged from £25 up. A top rider might get £500 or £1000. It all depends what section you're riding in, novice or open. It could be £25 up to about £1500. Sometimes you might lose and end up with some sort of injury – sick, sore, sorry, no money, back to work again. I was in Winton one time when a bloke called George Williams came over from America to ride in the Australian championship, and he ended up selling his saddle for £500 to get back to America. He auctioned his saddle and some idiot bought it for £500. That was big money in those days for a saddle. I always had my own saddle.

Sometimes I used to run into a mate, but most of the time I used to be travelling on my own. I was a very independent sort of a person, still am today I suppose. There was one bloke I knew, a feller called Wally Mailman from Queensland. He was Australian champion bulldogger, Wally. There were a few other young fellers – Buddy Tyson was riding, mainly in the southern area around South Australia – but there weren't very many. A few would come in and ride in the novice, but they were like me, they didn't follow it seriously, just rode whenever the rodeo came through. It's a young man's game and a mug's game with it I think, unless you're a top rider. My brother Gilbo was a top rider. He won the Australian championship buckjump at Alice Springs.

I knocked around for a couple of years, droving here and there, boxing and following the rodeos. I called in to see my father at Elliott a couple of times, and he got me a job on a place called Alcoota Station, a hundred miles north-east of Alice Springs. I was probably in my early twenties.

A feller called Bill Bonnings gave me a lift from Elliott into Alice Springs, where I made some enquiries and met Lou Leahy, one of the owners of Alcoota Station. He said, 'Righto young feller, come with me to Alcoota.' So off I went to Alcoota and when I got there to my surprise I bump into my best friend, Frankie Byrne, and a bloke called Archie Sturt who was also from Moola Bulla. I hadn't seen Frank since the day he left Beagle Bay.

**Frank Byrne:**   My father sent money to Beagle Bay all the time I was there for my education. One day Father McGinley told me, 'You've got to go to your father now.' That's when I left school. That was a hard trip too, because I was on my own. There was no other fellers on that trip.

They left me at a place called Rockhole out from Halls Creek, the same place Charlie went to, at Joe Williams' little shack there. Joe Williams was a hawker, and the people used to come to him to cash their cheques for flour, tea and sugar. He made a lot of money out of it.

Joe took me from there to Birrindudu in his little jalopy. Him and Oliver Booty – he was one of the old half-caste fellers, old Frederick Booty's son, and he knew the country really well. At that time when they took me there, there was no road, only the wheel tracks. My father was the manager and head stockman on Birrindudu Station. When I got there they were out at Wallamunga Waterhole getting a mob of bullocks ready for droving to Wyndham, and that's the first time I met my father, my real father.

I never felt like he was my father, but I suppose he was. As we worked along it happened that I couldn't get on with him. He was a good man, but there it is again, I lost my family and I couldn't get on with him. We never had an argument or anything but he knew I couldn't get on with him so he told me to go next door, to a place called Inverway Station. I worked there for I don't know how many years. When you're a young feller you don't care what job you got or how long you're there for – you're young and you just want to go and work.

I know I came to Napperby Station after Inverway, when I was seventeen or eighteen. Napperby was good, same as any other station. You're there to work and you get on well. People used to tell me I worked too hard, but that was all that made me feel right. And mainly I wouldn't stay too long in the one place – for a year, maybe more, and then go to another place. We were lucky in those days too. There was always a job there, they always wanted men and we were willing to work. We were experienced cattlemen and horsemen.

We had good teachers. When I worked on Inverway I had a good teacher, an old feller by the name of George Hamilton who was a sort of uncle to me. He was a very good rider. He taught me everything I know: cattlework, horse breaking, everything about station work, fencing or yard-building, all that.

After Napperby I went to Bushy Park, then Alcoota. At Alcoota when I met Charlie again I was working the stock-camp. I couldn't have been there too long, maybe a year, before Charlie came.

There were seven or eight blokes in the stockcamp. Turning back the years, everywhere we worked Aboriginal stockmen were the best ringers. Blackfellers were top cattlemen. They used to gather up the cattle in no time. And branding cattle! They used to brand hundreds, thousands, every year, and the sweat would pour out of the poor buggers.

It wouldn't take much to keep them. The tucker that they used to eat was corned beef and damper, put out on a bit of a hessian bag, cups for maybe twenty blokes – they were big camps then – and a drink of tea, maybe one spoonful of sugar in it.

And the pay – no pay. One pair boots, one hat, one trouser, one shirt, maybe a couple of blankets and a camp sheet, that's the pay. Stick of tobacco a week, and they used to work from daylight to dark.

Those Aboriginal ringers, they used to get a kick up the behind, and I've seen fellers who'd been hit over the head with hobble chains, things like that. It was just an everyday thing on some places.

There's one thing I can say about my father, he never had an argument with a blackfeller in his life. He used to like them, and they used to like him, and they'd work for him. You could go and ask any of those old blackfellers that worked on Birrindudu with my old man. He never used to tell them much because they knew what to do anyway.

Cattlework, it's a very good thing for young fellers. It gives them a start in life. You're disciplined, you get plenty of discipline. That's mainly why I say it's good for the young fellers. And of course it's the thing that we wanted to do from kid-time, because we were born in the station I suppose, and that was the life.

We were that fit in those days, we used to do anything; we'd knock off and still play hop, step and jump. You never see these things now. We used to be competing against one another all the time, we didn't stop. Anything we did was a competition, whether it was broncoing, riding horses, breakin' in – all the time it was a competition to see who's the best. We always wanted to be the better man than the other feller. Our life was pretty good, no complaint about them sort of things. There wasn't much money in it, but still it was the thing that we liked.

If I had to turn back the clock I'd go back to the same

thing again. We had a good life on the station. It's a marvellous life, a healthy life.

**Charlie:**   Of all the places that I worked, Alcoota was a really good station. Lou Leahy used to own the place, Leahy Brothers I think it was; and old Bill Turner, Charlie Perkins' step-brother, was the manager. He was a part-Aboriginal bloke and a great man.

I worked there for probably twelve months. Frankie Byrne, myself, Archie Sturt, and a few full-blood Aboriginals: Walter, Ned, Harold, Tommy, Bert, and I just forget the other bloke's name. I must admit, up until today, they were the best people I ever worked with. They were really top blokes, you didn't have to ask them to do anything. They knew exactly what they had to do.

It was really good there because Bill Turner was an Aboriginal feller and he knew how to work with Aboriginal people. Old Bill he's still alive, I think he's about seventy-eight or something like that. His wife Peggy was a wonderful woman. They always used to invite us to the manager's house for a feed. Bill and Peg were great people. I still see their kids. I worked with Barbara Cox, Bill Turner's daughter, for about two years with the Land Council.

Frank became head stockman on Alcoota, and about that time I saw an ad in the newspaper advertising for a horsebreaker on a place called Mt Dare, just near the Northern Territory border, on the South Australian side. Ted Lowe was advertising for a horsebreaker. I answered the ad and I got the job, so I took the train, the Ghan, down from Alice Springs to the railway siding at Abminga, where I was picked up and taken to Mt Dare Station.

When I got to Mt Dare, Ted Lowe just looked at me. You could see him thinking, Oh God, this is only a young feller, I wonder what he knows about breaking in horses. But he gave me the break. I broke in four pure-bred Arab stallions, using a method Joe Atkinson taught me, the real slow way. It's hard to explain, but you treat them like a kid, just taking them slowly, talking to them all the time, bagging them down, lunging them, picking their feet up one by one. Those four horses took me about three weeks to break in. Ted Lowe was very impressed with my work, so he gave me a job breaking in horses for the stockcamp.

There are lots of different ways of breaking in horses. It's a lot to do with the horse, and a lot to do with the amount of work you give them. Some horses are quieter than others, just like human beings – you meet good-natured horses and bad-tempered horses. On the stations they never broke in horses until they were three or four years old, and if you've got, well, what I call a mongrel horse, a bad-tempered horse four or five years old, it's hard. It's different in the southern states. A horse develops quicker and grows bigger in the soft country with plenty of feed than on a station. A three-year-old horse bred on a station in the Kimberley or the Northern Territory might be half the size of a two-year-old down south. That's probably why they used to break them in at three and a half, four years old.

I handled those four thoroughbred stallions the way I watched Joe Atkinson do it. When Joe Atkinson used to catch a horse he used to have a short rope, about ten foot long, and he'd put this rope round the colt or filly and leave it in the yard with another quiet horse. Then he'd put the horse out and grab hold of the rope with a bit of wire, and once he got hold of that rope he started mastering the horse. I've seen Joe Atkinson put a rope around a horse about four years old, and in a day he'd be riding him. That's how good that method is.

I would put a halter on them one by one, and just grab them by the halter and bag them down with a sugar bag tied on a bit of a stick until they quietened down. Usually they quieten down in a day. Next day I take each horse one at a time.

I put a saddle on one, and a bridle with a bit, let him run around. Next day I mouth him on a lunge, pull him gently to one side and then the other, make sure that he's looking at me all the time, and then I bag him down again. The third day I jump on him and ride him around the yard, then take him outside. Once you get him going he goes out to the stock-camp, and they do the rest there – teach him how to gallop, how to chase cattle and all that sort of thing. The more work you give them the better they turn out. You can do a rough job, say ten horses in a week, and in a month's time they turn out good horses because they've got plenty of work for them. You can do them quicker again, but then you've got to knock them down, and that's not the right way of doing it.

When you break a horse in you got to show him that you're master. Doesn't matter how you break 'em in, quick way, easy way or any way. The first thing you do is teach that horse that you're the master of him, and as soon as you teach him that, I suppose in one way he respects you and he more or less obeys you. That's the most important thing you got to tell him, make sure that you're the master of that horse.

If I was in a hurry to break in horses for a station, say they were short of horses for the stockcamp, I just put them through the crush and then I put what they call a spider on them, hobble all their feet up, front and back, so they can't kick or strike, and let them out of the crush, four at a time. Once they go out you can do whatever you like with them. You can jump on them, anything. It's the quickest way, but it's the hard way. You can break in about ten or fifteen a week.

If we ever got a horse that kept bucking or we couldn't catch him outside, we used to put a rope on the ground for him, catch him by the front leg or back leg, front leg the best, and he'd fall over a few times, and after a while he knows and then you can catch him. If he was a bucking horse, you'd ride him every day until you get the buck out of him. I wouldn't say it's cruel, if you know what you're doing. Especially when you're out in the bush, you know you've got to train the horse the best way you can.

Anyway I broke in twenty-five, maybe thirty horses all up, I just forget how many it was, and I got a job in the stockcamp at Mt Dare with a great old mate of mine, Alec Hussin from the Gulf Country. It was the same work as on other stations, mustering and branding. Mt Dare was a very interesting place for me because it's all tableland gibber country and hardly any grass, yet they breed fat cattle there. The country must be very sweet around that area.

In that stockcamp we had a bloke who was a Kiwi. I nearly smashed him up because one morning I woke up and here he was urinating in the Aboriginal stockmen's tea.

I said to him, 'What the fuck are you doing that for, mate? What do you think you are?'

'Oh,' he said, 'I'm sick of these blacks. The bastards ought to be shot.' We had a big argument and I couldn't talk to that bloke any more. The head stockman was there then, and he just said to me, 'It's none of your business, why don't you just shut your mouth?'

At the end of that mustering season we had a break, and when I went back to Mt Dare after the mustering season there was a feller called Bill Coolie who was contract mustering brumbies there. They were supposed to have about 6000 head of cattle there, if I can remember rightly. They had about 4000 head of brumbies on top of that. They had to get rid of them. Bill Coolie had maybe 2000 head of brumbies rounded up when the market ran out in Adelaide where they were selling these brumbies. They didn't know what to do with them.

So they shot a few and then they said, 'Oh bugger this, it's costing us too much in bullets.' Then Rex Lowe, Ted Lowe's son, attached two truck springs either side of the end of the race, sharpened them all up, and started galloping the brumbies through the race. He had the springs down at stomach level and as all the horses were galloping through, the sharp springs cut their stomachs open. The horses were galloping out, kicking and bucking, poor things, with their guts hanging out. They went for about half a mile before they dropped and slowly died.

When I saw this I said to the blokes, 'Bugger this, I'm not going to see this sort of thing happening, I'm off.' I went over to Rex and I said, 'I'm finished.'

He said, 'Why?'

I said, 'Why? I don't like that what you're doing.'

The rest of the guys followed me. They said, 'Yeah, we're all finishing up too.'

We all got paid off, and we were lucky that Rex gave us a lift back to Abminga railway siding. We caught the train there. I don't know whether it was the goods train or the Ghan, but anyway we got back to Alice Springs.

It was in Alice Springs that time that I met Valerie Stokes, her name was then. I was staying with some people next door to where she was living with her mother Clara Stokes and Clara's husband, old Dan Kennedy. Val was only seventeen years old and she was a very pretty girl. We used to look at each other over the fence as young people do, and then one day I managed to ask her for a date and that was it. I still remember the movie that night, it was called *The Fastest Gun Alive*.

Val and I were together for twenty-eight years. She was always a very attractive woman, never drank or smoked, always a nice person. That's why I fell in love with her. She's one of these persons you can't fault really. She reared eight kids, and the first few years we were together she used to wash all the nappies by hand until we managed to buy a washing-machine.

●

Valerie McAdam is a warm, soft-spoken woman. She lives in the Adelaide suburb of Elizabeth in a house filled with her children's sporting trophies and photographs, and alive with a constant flow of children and grandchildren. Her immediate response to the question, 'What was Charlie like when you met him?' was, 'Oh, he was lovely. He was tall, good-looking, always dressed smartly. There was no drinking in those days.'

Val is the youngest of three sisters. Her mother was an Arrernte woman from Yamba Station, out of Alice Springs. Her father was the son of a Samoan woman and was born in Tennant Creek. Val was born at Hamley Bridge, near Gawler, while her father was stationed there with the army during World War II, but the family moved back to Alice Springs when she was three years old. Like Charlie, Val was taken away from her family without any warning.

**Val McAdam:**    I was in Grade 3 when Welfare took us away. They just took us from where we were standing – no time to get our clothes, nothing, just told us to get in the back of the car. Our parents had no say. We were a family, but they just took us away.

I was about seven years old when that happened. We were sent to school in Adelaide to live with one woman in a private home. There were about four girls from Alice and three girls from Adelaide. She was like an old sergeant in the army. You had to do everything right. She was very strict.

I went to Blackwood Primary School, then Mitcham High School. We had no contact with our parents. If they were allowed to write I don't know, we had no word from them and we weren't allowed to go back there for holidays. I was about fifteen years old when this old girl looking after us down here died. They sent us back to our parents then, if we still had parents. My mum was still alive.

Margaret is my first child. She was three months old when I met Charlie. Margaret was born on 27 October 1958, then Greg our son was born on 18 February 1961. Pamela's birthday is 18 February 1965; Elizabeth, 20 April 1966; Gilbert, 30 March 1967; Michelle, 21 September 1969; Adrian, 12 March 1972; and Ian, 20 November 1973.

In 1961 I went out to Lake Nash with the two little kids, Margaret and Greg, to join Charlie. Greg was a baby then. It was pretty rough, but Charlie built a bit of a shack there and I liked it out there. The kids enjoyed it too I think. Charlie was away a lot. He used to do all the jobs, fencing and fixing bores and all that sort of thing. We stayed at Lake Nash about six months, and when the mustering season started we came back into town.

**Charlie:**   When I first met Val I had a week or two off and then I saw an ad in the paper: HORSEBREAKER WANTED AT LAKE NASH. Lake Nash was one of the biggest stations in the Territory, 160 miles west of Mt Isa on the Queensland border. I wrote a letter to the manager telling him my experience, and ten days later I got a letter back accepting me. Actually, I knew a bloke from Beagle Bay, maybe six, seven years older than me, that feller called Martin Trankilino who married my cousin Lou Lou. He recommended me to the manager and I got the job. I flew out to Lake Nash on Conellan Airways.

The manager was a feller called Gordon Jago. He was very impressed with my work breaking in horses and asked me if I wanted to stay and work on the stockcamp.

I said, 'I'd really appreciate that.'

'Okay,' he said, 'you've got a job.'

At the time, Martin Trankilino was running the camp. Frank Byrne had left Alcoota and he was there too. We did one droving trip all together. There were four of us, all West Australians: Martin Trankilino, Frank Byrne, myself, and a feller from Balgo, Johnny Ray – Jimaru is his blackfeller name. We took a mob of spayed cows from Lake Nash to Dajarra. Martin Trankilino is a man of many talents, a drover, saddler, yard builder and mechanic, and he taught us a lot. I think I worked with him for about twelve months, and then he decided to start up his own droving plant, which he did. He recommended me to the manager to run the stockcamp. 'If you want a bloke, Charlie McAdam's there. He's a good man and he'll do the work for you.'

Val was in Alice with the two kids, and I decided to come back and pick her up and take her to Lake Nash with me. There was no accommodation for married men, so I built a tent and a bough shed [an open shelter with a roof of leaves and branches] to keep the tent warm and for a shade area. We always had plenty to eat; we had our own beds and the kids had a cot, but it was on the ground and everything, dirt floor. I didn't want my kids to grow up like that. We had a little wood stove and Val cooked there, and washed the clothes in a 44-gallon drum, no washing-machine, and for light at night we used to pump up the tilly lamp. The tilly lamp was a kerosene thing, one of those lanterns with wires around the light. We used to fill it up with kero and start it by using methylated spirits, and when it was hot I would sort of pump it up and it threw a really good light. I made a shower out of a canvas with holes in it, and we used to boil up water for the kids to shower behind the tent, on a bit of a wooden floor or a sheet of tin or something, to keep them out of the mud. The water used to run behind somewhere down the drain. We lived pretty rough out there. I didn't believe in Val and the kids living like that, and it wasn't fair to them when I went out on the stockcamp, that's why I sent them back to Alice Springs. I didn't want my kids to grow up in those conditions. I've been through it.

Margaret used to play around the tent. We had a great big dam alongside of us, and it was a marvellous thing – I had a blue heeler bitch, we used to call her Biddy, and when that kid used to go near the dam Biddy would pull her away from it. One day Val and I were sitting in the bough shed and I said to her,

'Have a look at this.' Every time Margaret would go near the dam the dog would push her back. She was hitting the dog and screaming and she's saying, 'Mum, look at this Biddy! She won't let me in the water.'

'That's good! You're not allowed to go in that water!'

When we had that dog in Alice Springs, later on, no one could get near the kids. Nobody. One day when Greg was a little boy asleep in his cot, the copper from Lake Nash came around looking for me to give him a hand to load up to go back out to the station. When the copper got near the cot that dog grabbed him by the leg of the trousers. He was yelling, 'Charlie! Charlie!'

I stood at the door. 'What's the matter?'

He said, 'Look at this bloody dog of yours!'

I said, 'Well, that's what you get for going too near that kid. She won't let anybody near, only me or Mum.' She was a good dog. I used to take her out on the stockcamp. You can't beat a good cattle dog when you're working cattle.

One time, an old dingo bitch came to the dam to get a drink of water. That old dog of mine got stuck into her. When I saw that dingo I could see she had pups. I called Biddy away and let that poor bugger have a drink of water, and then away she went. I followed her that afternoon when it got cool, and I found where the pups were and I knocked them on the head. Plus I shot her. It used to be a pound in those days, the dog scalp.

Eventually I lent Biddy to a family to breed some pups and she got poisoned. They didn't look after her. I wasn't very happy about that.

Lake Nash was owned by Queensland National Bank. After a while the manager, Gordon Jago, resigned and his son-in-law, a feller called Arthur Jones, took over the management.

The Aboriginal people were camped about 500 yards away from the station. They had tin shacks and they were sleeping

under old bough sheds there. The Alyawarre mob had a different system to ours, because men wouldn't approach women
during the day, never – even husbands and wives, they'd
never mix during the day. Women stayed on their own and men
on their own. I think that Law extended from Agadagada
north to Utopia.

Lake Nash was a good place to be. We used to get fish all the
time, mainly yellow belly, out on the cattle run. The lake itself
was never dry but it was part of the people's drinking water too,
so we usen't to let cattle in there. We didn't want to stir it up. The
cattle and horses used to drink well water.

Out on the run we'd drive a mob of cattle through a couple of
foot of water, so they'd stir it up and all the fish would come up.
We used to get heaps of them like that. The people at Lake Nash
used to fish 'em out. They had big wire-netting traps too.
They used to put a bullock bone in there and fish would go in
there overnight and get caught in there, and every morning the
people would get three or four fish. Towards the end of the time
I was there the water out on the run was getting muddy from all
the shifting of cattle, and the water was going dry.

They were good people at Lake Nash. They had a very
good friendly relationship with Arthur Jones and old Gordon
Jago. Most of the people were all right, but in the stockcamp
there were always a couple of blokes who were stirrers. They said
they knew what was right for them, and I suppose they did, but
they used to stir the other blokes up so that they wouldn't
work. I would send them out for a muster and they'd only do
half of it and come back with the first thirty or forty head of
cattle they saw – things like that. It was only a couple of
blokes, otherwise they were good men. I suppose I shouldn't
speak of them, they're dead now.

I had the job there as the head stockman. I must admit, as I
said early in my story, I'd been poisoned by white people
saying that I wasn't a blackfeller, I was a yellerfeller, and all that

sort of rubbish. When I took the camp over I had twenty-four full-blood Aboriginal people working for me. This Lake Nash mob weren't very cooperative, and I suppose in my young days I was one of those smart bastards, thought I was a white man. I eventually got rid of two, three, four, five – just kept sacking and sacking them because they wouldn't do what they were told.

Towards the end of the year we had about 1500 head of steers at a place called Number Seven Bore ready to be delivered to Martin Trankilino, who was going to drove them to Dajarra. In those days we had to nightwatch them, to break them in so that when the drovers took them over they were quiet, ready to be watched at night. I handled them with about seven Aboriginal blokes but when we got all these cattle together two fellers, both the troublemakers, walked off from there. They used to always stir the other Aboriginal workers, and the other blokes followed them. I was looking after the cattle by myself and not one of these blokes came back. I couldn't leave the cattle there.

A young lad, a feller called Ronnie Mahoney, said to me, 'Hey Charlie, them blokes said they're not going to watch tonight because you got a yard just there.'

I said to him, 'You tell them that even though there's a yard we gotta get these cattle broke in for the drover.'

He went back out and told them blokes. They said, 'Nah, we're not gonna watch.' So anyway, we watched those steers all night, just the lad and I. We held them together. In the morning I was boiling with temper, I know. I had a .38 revolver. So I loaded this revolver and I rode over to the camp and said to them, 'What the fuck's going on here?' And that more or less started them off.

They said, 'Oh, you're a cheeky yellerfeller, eh? We'll give you a hiding.'

I said, 'Yeah, righto.'

I jumped off my horse and that's when the fight started. I knocked two of them out and one feller Mundy I hit with a water canteen. He was the instigator. The canteen was half full of water and I picked it up and I knocked him on the head.

Martin Trankilino raced over when he saw the fight starting. He said, 'Whoa, whoa Charlie! Don't do that, you'll kill the man!'

I said, 'What do you think I'm trying to do?' If I'd hit him a second time I might have busted his head open. Just as well Martin was there.

The other blokes wanted to fight me so I picked up my .38 and fired it in the air. They took off walking back towards Lake Nash. I thought, Will I follow these bastards? And I thought, No, I'd better not, otherwise I'll be in trouble. Away they went. Luckily Martin was camped maybe a mile away from where the main stockcamp was, and he brought his men over and took over the cattle.

When they got to the station the men told the manager and the police, 'Charlie's running amok out there, he was going to shoot us.' At Lake Nash they had a police station with one policeman and two or three trackers, in case there was tracking to be done, somebody lost, something like that. Trackers in those days had better living conditions than the rest of the people. Even if it was a shed there was a shower and toilet in it, usually right by the police station. The policeman was stationed at Lake Nash because his area took in all those places now, up around Agadagada, Utopia, right back to Alcoota. That was his run. Then there was a policeman at Avon Downs who did the northern side of it. They more or less worked together. They had a big area to cover.

The policeman came out. 'What's goin' on, Charlie?'

I said to him, 'Well, I'll tell you the story. We've got 1500 head of steers here ready to be delivered to this drover feller, and all

I want to do is break them in, you know, nightwatch 'em at night, and these fellers refuse to give me a hand to watch 'em.'

I explained my situation. He took me into the police station and I had to make a statement there, and he had all seven blokes in the cell there with him. He said, 'Righto you blokes, now you tell me your story.'

In the end the copper said, 'Those steers are worth a lot of money and you blokes should have stayed there and given Charlie a hand to quieten them down.' And then he said, 'Pity Charlie never shot the whole lot of you bastards.' That's what the copper said. I felt sorry then.

I suppose it was the responsibility, I don't know. Fifteen hundred head of steers, they were worth a few thousand pounds then, and I had watched them all night on my own with just the young lad. It was just over those bloody cattle. Plus the fact that when I was a young feller growing up I was more or less poisoned with people saying that I wasn't a blackfeller and all that sort of thing – that made me cocky in my young days.

That feller Mundy that I had a fight with was dumb – he couldn't talk – but he was one of those blokes who used to do the stirring. He could hear all right, he'd give me the sign language and all that sort of thing. He and the other two blokes that I mentioned all talked together. All Aboriginal people have their own sign language, and they could talk pretty well. Funny thing about that poor feller Mundy – he went to church one day and he reckons God made him talk. He told me that he went to church and the minister was standing there and he put his hands over his head and told him, 'Righto Mundy, get up and say, Hullo everybody.' And he got up and said, 'Hullo everybody,' and he couldn't believe he could talk. So he tells me now. He's still learning to speak now. He's still there on Lake Nash.

The Aboriginal people didn't want to work for me any more because they reckoned I was cheeky. The manager warned me, 'The company's not very happy with you, they're thinking about sacking you, but we'll give you another go.'

The following year I got about twelve part-Aboriginal and whitefellers to come to the camp. I had two Aboriginal fellers who were really good blokes still working for me as horse-tailers. At Lake Nash their record of branding was between eleven and twelve thousand head of cattle every year. We increased our branding to 16 000 that year.

At the end of the season I got a letter from the managing director or someone congratulating me and saying that I was doing a very good job. I continued on as the head stockman there for another two or three years, and after the first year I was getting round about two to four hundred pounds bonus each year.

●

The Alyawarre people of Lake Nash saw Charlie, the head stockman, a man from another country and a yellerfeller, as marginally less foreign than the non-Aboriginal proprietors of the station. The Alyawarre were a politically aware people engaged in their own long struggle. Hunted from their land to the west of the lake by the pastoralists, particularly in the 1920s, they had settled down on the station near their sacred lake Ilperrelhame and become the skilled labour force of the cattle station. In 1949 the stockmen went on strike and succeeded in negotiating a cash wage for the first time: £2 a month and free tucker.

Charlie's arrival at Lake Nash in 1960 was a time of increased agitation for equal wages by Aboriginal stockmen. Since World War II there had been stirrings of change in the northern cattle industry, partly because of increased Aboriginal awareness of the worth of their labour during the labour shortage of the war years.

Charlie, bound up in his own personal struggle and the demands of raising a young family, made a major decision.

**Charlie:**    I really liked Lake Nash and I wanted to stay there, but Valerie was living in Alice Springs with the kids. I had a little car, a Ford Prefect I bought in Alice, that's how I used to get up and down as much as I could. It was five or six hours on the dirt road. Before I bought the car I used to fly back on Conellan Airways. They used to have a weekly service from Alice Springs to Mt Isa, dropping off mail to stations on the track to Mt Isa, then they'd collect mail in Mt Isa and fly back to Alice the same day.

A little while after, Valerie had another child. We called him Graham Frederick. I saw him when he was born, but then I left and drove back out bush to take a mob of cattle from Lake Nash to Dajarra, and the police got in touch with me just out of Eurandangie. He was dead of pneumonia, the poor little bugger.

I worked on for a while but I kept thinking to myself, I've got to settle down, my wife's in Alice Springs with my kids and I'll have to resign. Plus I had to look for a better paying job once I had a family. Anyway I resigned from Lake Nash and went back to Alice Springs to my wife and two kids.

# Living
## in Alice

**Charlie McAdam:**     MY FIRST JOB in Alice Springs was driving a sanitary truck, emptying out toilet pans and pumping out urine tanks and that. I lasted maybe a week or two and I resigned, because it was too dirty and too stinking and I didn't like taking back filth to my wife and kids.

Valerie and I had ten children. The first one was young Margaret and the second was young Gregory, and then the little boy Graham who passed away. And then we had Elliot, and he was in an accident and was killed. He was going to school. He jumped out of the bus, slipped around in front of the bus and got hit by a car. That was the saddest time of my life. I just could not believe it. From the time he got killed – even today when I'm on my own, I just sit down sometimes and I think about him and I start to swallow – I start to choke just thinking about him. Tears come out of my eyes. I've never ever forgotten him.

After Elliot came Pamela, Elizabeth, Gilbert, Michelle, Adrian, and Ian. While they were growing up Valerie used to encourage the girls to play hockey and different sports, and I used to concentrate on encouraging those boys to play football, cricket and whatever.

All the time my wife and I were living together we had a great life growing those kids up. I must say this – every one of my children, boys and girls, represented the Northern Territory in all sorts of sports, in football, soccer, hockey, netball. They participated in all the sports they could play in.

Val and I always encouraged them to play sports to keep them away from trouble and we were both very strict with them. They never ever went hungry. I always said to myself, When I grow up and have children they won't go through what I went through, and they didn't.

People often ask me, 'Where do those kids of yours get their sporting ability from?'

I say, 'Well, I don't know. My wife was a top sportswoman, very good at hockey.' Val played in the Centralian hockey team, as well as playing softball and basketball. In my earlier days when I came back from Lake Nash and got a job in Alice Springs I played a bit of football there with Rovers Football Club. I just played to keep fit and I enjoyed myself, but I was never a champion. I think I was a bit too bad-tempered to play good football.

I was always interested in horseracing and used to go out to the track at Alice Springs all the time. When I was at Lake Nash I swapped an old drover feller a couple of bronco horses for a thoroughbred gelding. He was going contract mustering and he said, 'Give me a couple of bronco horses and I'll give you a racehorse.' He was a well-bred horse but they couldn't get him into the barrier. He was a real yang-yang mongrel bastard. Still, he was a good-looking thoroughbred horse, a yellow bay with two white hind feet and a baldy face, but he had beautiful conformation. He had Coronation Boy blood in him, and anything that Coronation Boy threw could win races.

I worked him on the stockcamp at Lake Nash, and one year I took him to Eurandangie and won a race there, and then I lent him to a feller called Mace Clancy to take to Mt Isa. He won his race and Mace Clancy offered me £400 for him. Four hundred pounds was a lot of money in those days so I sold him. I had a couple of horses after that. I took them to Rockhampton, and Townsville and then back to Alice, but Whitefoot was the best racehorse I ever had. In the end I got to a point where I was sort of square and that's when I gave the racing away.

Once we moved into Alice Springs the jobs and the years sort of ran into each other. My next job was with the Department of Works on a bore maintenance gang. The boss was a feller called Tom Coles, the son of Mabel Coles who had Mabel Downs, just out of Halls Creek. My mother used to work for the Coles many years ago. Old Tom was very pleased to have me working with him because my mother used to do the housework for Mrs Coles and look after Tom and his brother Sandy. We used to talk about different things round Springvale and Halls Creek. He was a funny old man but a very good old bloke to work with.

That job took me everywhere. We used to maintain bores as far out as Giles in Western Australia, Amata in the north of South Australia, up to Lake Nash and Tennant Creek, and right up to Tanami out in the desert. We covered almost every stock route in the whole of the Northern Territory. It was a good job, and good money. Even though I was away from my family, at least I knew I was working and supporting them.

One time we were in the desert out from Giles and we pulled up for lunch under a desert oak tree. I saw an old Pit-jantjatjara bloke waving to us from under a tree further up. He was perishing for water. We gave him a drink of water and chucked a bit of water over him. I couldn't understand him and he couldn't understand me at first, but after a while he took us across to a place where there were half a dozen families without water. The water had all dried up there. We radioed the Department of Works and they radioed Amata, and they sent a truck out with a nurse to pick those people up.

After a couple of years I got itchy feet, so I went droving again. A feller named Dick Smith offered me a job as a boss drover, because he had two plants. We took a mob of cattle from Eva Downs on the Barkly Tableland to Camooweal. Frank Byrne was with us. We had some really good blokes with us, Pitjantjatjara people from Mt Ebenezer Station near Ayers Rock. They could hardly speak English but they were good men, very reliable.

Along the track, at a place called Lawn Creek, two police officers came out to check on some horses that had been stolen. While they were there, looking round to see if we had any stolen horses, they saw where we killed a killer. They said to Frank, who was doing the cooking, 'Who killed this killer?'

'Oh, Charlie.'

The copper said to him, 'By Jesus, it seems to be pretty fat.'

'Oh yeah,' Frank said to him. 'We've got some pretty fat cattle in amongst our cattle.'

The copper replied, 'I don't think so, mate.' He questioned me, and he tried to bluff me into saying that the cook told him I shot one of Alexandria's or Brunette Downs' bullocks, not one of ours. Actually, I'd be surprised if any drovers ever took killers out of their own mob, if there was an alternative. Drovers got paid by the number of live beasts they delivered.

A trucking company from Tamworth in New South Wales was carting the cattle from Camooweal into Mt Isa. One of the driver's family had died in Tamworth, and the boss offered me a job truck driving for him.

We did a couple of trips carting cattle from New South Wales to Alligator Creek and Charters Towers in Queensland, and back to Tamworth again. I teamed up with another feller there and he and I drove an old bomb Chev ute up the coast of

Queensland, right up through Cairns, Rockhampton and back down through Southport. This old bomb broke down there and I didn't have the money to fix it, so I went back to Tamworth. Keith, the boss of the trucking company, helped me out and paid my fare back to Mt Isa.

There was a job going for a horsebreaker on Headingley Station on the Northern Territory–Queensland border. I broke in about twenty or thirty horses and then I got another job droving with Clarrie Pankhurst. We picked up about five or six hundred head of bullocks at Marion Downs and took them to Winton. It was a really good trip, and a happy one with that. We had a couple of TI [Thursday Island] blokes there with us, a couple of Aboriginal fellers, myself, and two whitefellers. When we delivered the cattle in Winton I took the empty plant back to Lake Nash. On the way, the manager at a sheep station called The Grove offered us a job for ten days, and it was pretty handy because we gave our horses a spell. When we finished there I think I had about £40. I took the horses back to Lake Nash and then went back to Alice Springs. I was really glad to be back with my family.

Anyway, I lazed around there for maybe a week or two and I got a job working as a truck driver and a crusher operator with South Australian Industries, owned by an old feller called Ted Smith. Maybe two years later I got a job with Humes Pipes. A feller called Bert Fittock was the manager there. I started as a foreman and moulder. I did a fair bit of spot-welding there, making reinforcements for pipes and box culverts, and when Bert used to go away on holidays I used to run the place for him. It was very hard work because in those days all the concrete mixing and pouring was done by hand.

After I finished with Humes I worked with my father-in-law, Dan Kennedy, erecting road signs on the Northern Territory highways and all around the Alice Springs area, putting up identification signs to all the tourist places. We used to put up white guide posts on the road, and dip signs and grid signs as well.

Then I was employed with Alice Springs Town Council as a truck driver on a bitumen gang. We used to have a lot of fun because there were a lot of Aboriginal blokes working there. I used to mainly work with a feller called Nobby Salter. The foreman was a very good bloke, a feller called Snowy McIntyre. The rest of the gang was really happy-go-lucky, mainly Aboriginal employees.

In 1973 a feller called Georgie Bray asked me if I wanted a job with the Central Australian Aboriginal Legal Aid Service [CAALAS] in Alice Springs, which they were starting up at that time. Bobby Stewart and I were the field officers. There was Georgie Bray, Cathy Martin, Phyllis Harrison, and a girl called Francie – a white lady we employed there – and Snooky de Bois. The first lawyer for CAALAS was a feller called Jim Montgomery from Melbourne.

When I was with Legal Aid there was an alleged murder incident round Docker River in the Pitjantjatjara country. There were about four blokes involved in it. The police from Kulgera arrested them and took them into Alice Springs. As field officers, Bobby Stewart and myself went with the lawyer, Jimmy Montgomery, to assist with these four blokes. These poor fellers could hardly speak English. They just didn't know what they were there for or anything. It was a sad thing, because no one had any way of knowing whether they had done the wrong thing or not. They were acting according to their own Law in their own country.

When they went to court Bobby and I were there. The magistrate was Scrubby Hall. Everyone in Alice Springs knew Scrubby Hall. Scrubby asked these fellers whether they were guilty or not, and one of the old fellers, he just stood there, didn't know what to say.

Scrubby said, 'Mr So-and-so, how do you plead?' and there was silence.

The old feller scratched his head and looked around every-where, and finally he said, 'Ooh, I don't know, Boss,' he said, 'I think sometime I bleed through the nose.' My God. There was a bit of laugh, and hissing, people catching their breath, and silence. The magistrate dismissed the whole case in the end because those people could not understand English, they did not know what they were saying, they were really old tribal men. Everybody was laughing about it after the court case. Bobby and I had a bit of a laugh about it ourselves, but when you think deeply, it's not funny. It's just those people did not know the white man way of life, and the white man courthouse.

I could just imagine a few years back, back in the thirties and forties what the old people at home went through, the poor buggers. They could not speak English, could not understand white man's law, they had no lawyers, they had nothing. Very, very sad.

●

The Central Australian Aboriginal Legal Aid Service was set up in 1973 to provide proper legal representation for Central Australian Aboriginal people. It was preceded by Aboriginal legal services set up in Redfern in 1970, Adelaide in 1971, and Fitzroy in 1972. The original concept of setting up shopfront legal services for Aboriginal people was formulated by three young Kooris: Paul Coe, Gary Foley and Gary Williams. At the same time, the Aboriginal Medical Service Cooperative, established in Redfern in 1971, was to be the forerunner of more than sixty Aboriginal health services established tho-rughout Australia in the next twenty years.

These community-controlled services were endorsed by the new Whitlam government's policy of self-management for Aboriginal people, as opposed to assimilation. They became prime movers in achieving rights for Aboriginal people and formed an integral part of the political, social and economic development of communities. At the same time they were under enormous pressure as fledgling organisations working in the face of overwhelming need.

The struggle for Aboriginal rights, which had been constrained by isolation on reserves and the daily pressures of survival, developed into intense agitation in the '70s, spearheaded in part by a number of young, educated and highly articulate young Aboriginal men and women. This was a period when Aboriginal people across Australia asserted themselves in their own right, supported by the fundamental goodwill of a largely uninformed Australian population and limited financial assistance from governments.

A number of events distinguished this modern movement from earlier times. In 1967 over 90 percent of white Australians had voted yes to a referendum to include Aboriginal people in the census and to give the federal government power to legislate for Aborigines. In the same year the Federal Council of Australian Aborigines and Torres Strait Islanders (FCAATSI) was established. This was the first national organisation established and controlled by Aborigines.

In 1966 Charles Perkins had instigated the Freedom Rides in New South Wales, in which Aborigines and their supporters toured country towns protesting at segregation in hotels, swimming-pools and other public places. But the main event of 1966 was the walk-off by the Gurindji people from their jobs as stockmen at Wave Hill Station – part of a large pastoral lease held by the London-based Vestey group – and their demands for their land to be returned to them. After five years of negotiation the federal government paid Vestey to surrender some 3200 square kilometres at Watties Creek to the Gurindji. This walk-off was a landmark in the Aboriginal struggle, and marked a shift of focus from wages and living conditions to land rights and self-management.

In 1972 the Tent Embassy established on the lawns of

Parliament House in Canberra focused national and international attention on the plight of Aboriginal people. The embassy flew the new Aboriginal flag, designed in Adelaide in 1971, which symbolised the black people, the red earth, and the golden sun – the hope of a new day.

But despite these changes, problems remained. In Alice Springs, as in other places, the Aboriginal population made a disproportionate number of appearances in court, on charges ranging from drunkenness to serious assault. Police made arbitrary arrests, frequently beating those they detained. The conflict between Australian law and Aboriginal customary Law compounded the situation, resulting in some people being punished twice, once by the white court and again by community members.

**Charlie:** I really enjoyed working at CAALAS. It didn't last long, because some accounts didn't balance and the executive committee sacked us all. We were asked to reapply for the job but I thought, I'm not going to work for this mob after they sacked me, because I wasn't guilty of any foul play.

After that job with Legal Aid I got a job with McMahon Constructions as a loader operator, building a new sub-division called Sadadeen on the east side of Alice Springs. The blokes weren't very friendly because they were mainly all white people, and if you were an Aboriginal person working with them they wouldn't mix with you very much.

•

In the early years of their marriage, while Charlie's work alternated between jobs in Alice Springs and out bush, Val McAdam was often on her own raising the children.

**Val McAdam:** Charlie was away a lot. When he was working on the bore gang, that was the Department of Works

and Housing, he was out bush a lot, fixing bores and that –
sometimes two or three weeks a month. He was here about half
the time, I suppose. I had no help from anyone. I was by
myself.

I was working at the same time at the hospital, Alice
Springs hospital. In '57 I started there. They got me a job
there, cleaning and that sort of thing, as soon as I came back
from Adelaide. I worked there since Margaret was born, from
seven o'clock in the morning till four o'clock in the afternoon.

At night we used to have the table set and clothes all out, and
the kids would just get up in the morning and have a shower and
dress and go to school and I'd go to work then. After school they
used to go play and they all had little jobs to do around the
house. They all used to help each other after school, and they
didn't fight much. They all used to agree on decisions. Gilbert and
Adrian were the quiet ones. The kids knew what they had to do
and what they weren't allowed to do. They knew if they didn't do
it, when Charlie came home they'd get a hiding. And Charlie was
very strict with the kids. It was the way he was brought up I
think. But Charlie and I always agreed on the way we brought up
the kids. I wasn't as strict as Charlie was, but they knew how far
they could go with me too. During the week I'd just go to
work, that's all, and on the weekend if I got any time I might just
go and see my sister.

I never felt I missed out or anything. I used to enjoy the times
with my kids. My happiness was watching my kids running
around the house laughing.

In 1974 my family came down here from Darwin after
Cyclone Tracy, twenty-six of them in the backyard in cara-
vans. Charlie was in town at the time. They were here a
month, maybe more. My cousin's son's wife got mixed up
with all the mob in town, drinkin' and stuff, and one day she left
and never came back. She left behind her baby son, Ian. We
heard him crying in the caravan out the back. He just became

part of our family. He probably knows about it but he hasn't asked me about it.

**Pamela (McAdam) Reilly:**   We had a lot of chores to do. Mum used to do a roster once a week and stick it on the fridge. We had to wash the dishes, sweep and mop the floor, vacuum the carpet, clean our room out, do our washing, hang the washing out, water the trees. We had to stick to that roster and we all had the same amount of work to do so no one could complain. It was good.

   We had to do all the chores before we could go anywhere, or before any kids could come over, even in school holidays. One of us might try and get out of it, but we soon got straightened out when Dad got back – maybe it was because he was brought up strict, so that's the way he brought us up. Other kids used to roam the streets and do what they wanted to do. We had to be home by sundown, or else we'd be in big, big trouble. If we wanted to go out, we'd go to Mum first and then Mum would say, 'Go and ask Dad.' So Dad would have the final say. Mum wasn't soft, but she made it a little bit easier for us.

**Elizabeth McAdam:**   We are a really close family but there were a few fights, just among us kids, if the others didn't do their jobs. Gilbert hated washing up so he'd always try to get out of that, and the boys would always try and get out of picking up rubbish and cleaning up the yard. The girls were better at doing the jobs than the boys. Adrian would often try to find his way out of doing the jobs.

**Adrian McAdam:**   One thing that's always in my mind is the way Mum used to bring us up. We'd wake up in the morning and have our showers, then breakfast would be ready, toast and everything would be just there waiting for us, and then we'd be off to school. That wasn't just for two or three years, that was all the time we were at school, every day. When we got home we had to do the right thing, dishes and cleaning and all that sort of stuff, because she did the right thing for us. Living together in such a big family we had to help each other out.

●

The McAdam household was always full of people coming and going, just like a drop-in centre according to Pamela. Val recalls that when the children's friends would sleep over, there were bodies everywhere and feeding them was like feeding an army.

For a while Charlie coached a local cricket team, and on Saturdays after cricket, or during the week after work, he would take his family and friends out hunting in the F100. The kids and Val had mixed feelings about these expeditions.

**Val McAdam:**   I didn't like shooting that much. When he used to say, 'We're going shooting,' the kids used to scatter. 'Come on, let's go bush,' he'd say, and they used to run away. When the boys got older they used to take their friends out with them, and later on he used to take three or four grandchildren out shooting. The happiest time was when we were all together as a family. We used to have an F100 and pile all the kids in the back, all our kids and their friends.

**Pamela (McAdam) Reilly:**   It was just the waiting around, sitting out bush when you could be in town with your friends. Looking for the kangaroos – that was the longest part, looking for the kangaroos. No matter what, we used to always come back with a kangaroo. We used to stay out there until we got one. The F100 had a canopy top on the back. All the kids would sit in the back. If I went out bush with my family now, I suppose I could cook a kangaroo from the way Dad's shown us.

•

Greg saw hunting as a necessity to put food on the table.

**Greg McAdam:**  Dad had to go hunting for rabbits or turkeys or roos because we were a big family and Mum and Dad were always looking after other people's kids – we just didn't have the money to buy all the food from the shops.

I really enjoyed it initially, but I suppose when fun becomes a chore you sort of look at it differently. As I was getting older I used to have to go out with Dad on our own. I used to have to drive the car or do the spotting. I used to try to get out of it. We used to try to come home when the sun went down, and Dad would ask us what we'd been doing, so we'd always say we were at footy practice or sporting practice, which was always a way to get out of trouble. Regardless, we still had to get in the car and go, so it made no difference in the end anyway.

**Adrian McAdam:**  We'd play cricket on a Saturday, I used to play cricket with all the older guys, 'cause Dad was coaching at the time. We'd play all Saturday and then we'd go out bush Saturday afternoon and we'd virtually have the whole cricket team with us. We used to be sitting in the back of the truck and once he'd killed a kangaroo we'd jump off. Sometimes we'd go out in the F100 and spend the whole night out there.

We always came back with something to fill the freezer up. It was good. Dad taught us how to cut up the kangaroo because you have to do it right, especially back at home if the old people are watching. I learnt a lot from Dad and going out bush.

•

Bush trips and other adventures yielded a variety of pets: a calf, a succession of joeys, a pig and a wedge-tailed eagle. Charlie found the egg on a droving trip and hatched the eagle out bush. Val said the eagle just grew up with the kids.

**Greg McAdam:**   That eagle was an unreal bird. It wasn't as though we consciously trained it or anything. He used to flap along the ground and kick the footy with his claws, and if you booted it a long way he'd fly out and pick it up with his claws. He used to play with us, hide in the trees, swoop down. If he'd been gone for a couple of hours and we couldn't find him, Dad would come out and whistle out for him and he'd just come circling in the sky and fly in. He used to have a big cage out the back. Dad used to have a glove and he used to eat out of Dad's hand. He was really tame, that eagle.

   Eventually a couple of dogs died in the neighbourhood. They were poisoned but people said the eagle had killed them, so they just came and took him away, grabbed him upside down by the feet and carried him out like an old rooster.

●

There were close ties with the extended family, with Val's mother and sisters in Alice Springs and Charlie's family. There was a strong bond between the three brothers, the sons of Jimmy McAdam, and their families. Gilbert and Elliot visited in Alice Springs and Charlie took his children back to Halls Creek regularly.

**Pamela (McAdam) Reilly:**   Mum's mother was living in Alice Springs, over at Bloomfield in the Gap area. We saw a lot of them, and every time we'd go to Halls Creek we used to bring Dad's mother back. One time we brought her back and she was all dirty from the way she was living in Halls Creek, so we cut her hair and cleaned her up. Nanna – I can just see her now sitting outside, just being herself. Michelle and Adrian would tease her and she'd sing out, 'Oh, Charlie come and get these kids.' She was kind, a lovely lady. We didn't understand her language but Dad did. When she'd sing out to Dad if we were doing something wrong, she'd say our names in Kija. I was quite young, about eleven or twelve when she died.

**Elizabeth McAdam:** I think I was a bit scared of her. Mum used to say that I used to eat my grandmother's pituri [native tobacco] when I was little, and one time I got sick. I was always excited to see her again, to see all of them actually, it was really good. There were so many people in that family. My grandmother lived with us for six months once, but she didn't like it, she was getting homesick, and Dad ended up taking her back.

**Greg McAdam:** I remember Clara – Mum's mother – and Aunty Hetty – Charlie Perkins' mother – and the other old women taking us to get all the bush food, like yalkas [wild onions], langkwe [bush bananas], and a lot of other stuff. My grandmother and her friends used to take us out, sit down with the yalkas, and put them in the fire. My parents' upbringing was really special, really traditional. They had some sort of balance, the bush mob. I'm really proud that you only go back two generations and our people come from bush.

●

The pattern of days was sport and school, in that order, for the young McAdams, who showed an unusual aptitude for a wide variety of sports.

**Val McAdam:** They used to play games outside – golf, football, tennis – whatever they felt like, they played. It was just natural. On Saturday mornings I used to clean the house and then we used to walk a fair way to Traeger Park sports ground. No one was ever left behind – we always used to go to things together. I was usually pushing the pram along. We didn't have a car in those days. People would say, 'There goes Val and her tribe.' *(laughs)*

Margaret played competition hockey. The boys played soccer on Saturday mornings, Saturday afternoon they'd have football, Sunday they'd play something else. Gilbert used to play rugby Sunday afternoon, Adrian used to do a bit of boxing, Greg was cycling. The girls were playing netball, softball and basketball. Ian played football and soccer.

**Adrian McAdam:**    Sport was just something that we did. We were all family and we used to stick together and play together. We were always playing something in the backyard – if it wasn't soccer it would be cricket, if it wasn't cricket we'd be playing on the table-tennis table, basketball, football, anything really. We used to have a lot of stuff at home, the pool table, the table-tennis table, all those things, so we grew up on sports.

I suppose I learnt some of my skills in the backyard playing with my brothers and sisters and all my mates, because actually I smashed a few windows in the backyard. I certainly had to learn to control the ball after that.

I think we learnt some of our footy skills from going out hunting as well, just running around having a bit of fun, chasing joeys and rabbits.

Mum and Dad were good. They were always there. They were pretty strict and if we didn't do the right things we wouldn't be allowed to play sport on the weekend, which crucified us because that was our main thing.

**Pamela (McAdam) Reilly:**    If there was a notice there at school for anybody who wanted to represent the school in a particular sport we'd go for it, and then we'd go home and tell Mum and Dad how much it cost and they'd try and save up money. We went to Brisbane, Sydney, Canberra, all over the place, Perth, Hobart, Adelaide. There was always one kid going away on a sporting trip and that kid would come back and the next kid would go, so Mum and Dad sort of forked out thousands for us to play sport.

**Elizabeth McAdam:**  Me and Gilbert used to always go away together. Gilbert played football or cricket, so he would go away for the football and I'd go for the netball which was on at the same time.

We used to play so many games in the backyard, our family and all our friends. We used to play golf, tennis, cricket – you name it, we played it. It was really good. The boys or the girls would pick teams and we more or less swapped around, but we would never let Gilbert and Adrian play on the same team. We had to split those two, because they were really good. Greg had gone away to play football in Adelaide by that time.

**Charlie:**  Back in the '70s Greg was picked in the primary school football team from the Northern Territory. He was one of the few boys from Alice Springs that got picked. Most of the others were from Darwin.

When Greg came back he had a surprise for us. He got picked in the All Australian side. That was the greatest moment. Mum and I were very very proud of him. We just couldn't believe it, our son picked in the All Australian side. I can remember showing all my friends the gold medal he had: 'This is Greg's, you know, he got picked in the All Australian side.' That was the start of it. Every one of those kids represented the Northern Territory and most of them got picked for an All

Australian side. Ian is potentially a very good footballer too. He represented Alice Springs in a team that went to Darwin but he chose to do an apprenticeship and only plays football socially. And they're all good kids, really good kids. I was very lucky to have kids like that. Now that they're all grown up, most of them married up, I have fourteen wonderful grandchildren. I love 'em all.

Anyway, after a while I just got sick of working at McMahon Constructions. Some of them were nice fellers, but the rest of the gang – I don't know if they were snobby, racist, or what they were, but they just didn't want to mix. They just mixed with their own mates.

That was when I went to Ord River Station, back in the Kimberley. My brother Gilbo had a contract mustering the cattle from Ord River Station because that country was all flogged out, all eaten out, and they had to get rid of the stock from there to regenerate the place. They had something like fifteen to twenty thousand head of cattle on that property. I think that station is still in the process of regeneration. It's taken them years and years to make that country look good again. I went over there and worked with my brother. I was getting good money there with him.

While I was working there I got a letter from my wife. At the time I went to Ord River, things were not good between us. She wrote to me saying that if I stayed there I needn't bother coming back, and if I did go back she did not know what we were going to do. At the time she wrote me the letter she was a very sick woman, I think it was gallstones. She was very worried. I had a talk to my brother about what was happening at home with my wife and I, and he said, 'All right, the best thing for you is to go back there and see what you can do.'

Back to Alice Springs to my wife and kids. It wasn't a very happy atmosphere. There was something about us – well, I knew that before I got back. She wasn't very happy with me and

I wasn't very happy with her, even though I understand she was a very sick woman. She eventually had an operation. I stayed around there for a while. We tried to get on but we just couldn't, so in the end I decided to go back out bush again.

I got a job in the rural section of the Institute for Aboriginal Development. Yami Lester was the director there. Our job was to give the Pitjantjatjara people a hand to get rid of their TB and brucellosis cattle. A lot of those places had up to 3 percent TB and brucellosis in their herds. My area was mainly around Mimili, Fregon, Kenmore Park, Ernabella, Amata and Alpara. It was very interesting work. I used to work with the stock inspectors there. We used to test for TB and brucellosis, and whatever was showing positive we had to shoot them there, and burn the carcases.

I continued working on with a poor old feller called Ninga Stewart on Alpara Homeland. He had a few cattle there and he was in debt, so I more or less helped him out. He was very pleased and I was pleased to be able to help him.

•

The homelands movement began in northern and central Australia in the 1970s to establish living areas for extended family groups on their traditional lands. It was an Aboriginal initiative to counter the trend to fringe camps and towns. Homelands were set up on the Anangu Pitjantjatjara lands from 1976 onwards.

**Charlie:**  Next I went to Santa Theresa Mission. They reckoned they had about 800 head of cattle which belonged to the Church, and they wanted to get rid of them so they could restock with a new mob of cattle for the Aboriginal community. I ended up getting 1200 head of cattle in about three to four weeks.

At that time Aboriginal stockmen had a lot of problems.

Every pension day and payday blokes from Alice Springs used to come in, all their friends and relatives, and there were a lot of problems, grog problems of course. They were good men, but it was just the grog.

•

Alcohol emerged as a significant health problem for Aboriginal people after prohibition was repealed in the Northern Territory in 1964 and Western Australia in 1972. In some places it is used as currency. Although it affects a minority of Aboriginal people, it is a highly visible problem. Drunkenness accounted for one-third of Aboriginal arrests in 1988, in a population detained at twenty times the rate of the non-Aboriginal population nationally. In Western Australia in 1990 the arrest rate for Aborigines was forty-three times greater than for non-Aborigines.

There is no basis for the stereotype that Aboriginal people have a genetic predisposition to drunkenness and there are various theories for the overconsumption of alcohol. Drinking is at first a pleasurable group activity for people whose behaviour patterns are sociable and group-oriented. From colonial times there have been records of Aboriginal people learning drunken behaviour from Europeans. Heavy drinking was normal, even admired as a measure of manhood, in frontier areas, and drinking became an expression of equality with the white man. Drinking can also be an expression of defiance. As with non-Aboriginal people, alcohol can be used to counter feelings of boredom, powerlessness and loss of self-esteem. There are no indigenous rules about alcohol use, and in some areas traditional outlets for self-expression no longer exist. Relationships govern interactions between people, and in some relationships a request cannot be denied. Nor can the duties of gift-giving be avoided, and alcohol is a convenient gift. Added to these factors is the availability of alcohol: in some towns taxi drivers are known to provide a running tab, delivering alcohol to camps in return for Aboriginal pension cheques.

Initiatives to counter the problem are being made by Aboriginal communities and organisations, and range from prohibition on Aboriginal land to education and rehabilitation.

**Charlie:**   Towards the end of the muster we had about 1500 head of cattle in a paddock. I had to go into town for something, and when I got back the cattle were all gone. These fellers all got drunk and they let all the cattle go again. So we had to muster all over again, but it didn't take very long to get them all back because they were still together – maybe three to four days. Eventually we trucked them to Alpara.

I made a deal with Alpara, actually. I said to old Ninga Stewart, 'Look old feller, can we put these 1500 head of cattle in your property for agistment for about three months and we'll give you –' I think it was about 250 head of cows and calves – 'to pay for it. What do you think about that?'

He said, 'No worries, Charlie.' He was very happy about that because he knew me very well. I'd worked with him and he really liked me because I'd done the right thing by him before, I suppose.

So anyway we trucked them to Alpara, and they had to be there at least three months to fatten up and get strong, because they were pretty weak when we shifted them away from Santa Theresa. I was there caretaking, looking after the cattle – making sure they had water and all this sort of thing – and I had to count whatever I saw dead around the area. When I was at Alpara it was really good. I had two blokes with me there. Every morning we'd get up early, jump on our horses and ride the boundary to see where the cattle were. When the cattle all settled down I paid off the two blokes working for me and I stayed on for another couple of months, until the cattle fattened up a bit, and I trucked them to Adelaide. When I mustered 1500 head of cows and calves on Santa

Theresa they were really happy with me, and they paid me a $6000 bonus at the end.

After I came back from Alpara the only job I could get in Alice Springs was taxi-driving, and that was the year that we really split up. Val was working night-shift in the hospital and we hardly saw each other. Val and I were really happy for most of the time we were together. Unfortunately, it came to an end after twenty-eight years.

It was in 1987 that Val and I separated. I don't know why, but the last two or three years of our marriage we used to argue, argue over anything. Anything I said, she wouldn't agree, she'd jump down my throat. And whatever she'd say, I would disagree, and things like that.

It went on and on and on, until one day Val said, 'I'm going to Adelaide.' The kids were all pretty well grown up by then. Greg was living in Adelaide, and Val moved to Adelaide with Adrian, Michelle and Ian. She's still there today. I think that was the best move in the end.

She did not get in touch with me for maybe eighteen months to two years. One day she rang me up. She must have been thinking about me, poor thing, and I suppose she thought something good about me, even though the last three years of our marriage were not very welcome. I suppose she thought of the better days and rang me up.

'Oh, how are you going, Dad?' When I heard her voice I started to swallow – I cried on the phone. She said, 'Why don't you come to Adelaide and see us.' And I said, 'Well, that's the best thing I've heard, I'd love to see you and the kids.' Actually she only had a couple of the kids with her at the time; they were all grown up.

It was great to see my wife again and be friends again. Even though we are living apart now we're just as good friends as we were when we first met. Every now and then I go to see her. I'm invited to the place. We have some good old yarns and she takes me out, showing me different places in Adelaide, going shopping and all sorts of things. Not that I'm much of a one for shopping, but it's great to get together again. I'll never forget that phone call because I thought that after she dumped me she'd never ever talk to me, or I'd never see her again, but it was the other way around, thanks God.

# Traeger Park
# to the MCG

IN 1976 GREG McAdam represented the Northern Territory in the Under 16 Schoolboys State Football Carnival, and was picked for the All Australian team. Two Adelaide clubs showed interest in the promising young footballer, and at the age of fourteen he moved to Adelaide. Adjusting to city life can be difficult for any country teenager, and particularly for young Aboriginal men, but at the time his uncle Elliot McAdam was living in Adelaide and Greg was able to live with him. Elliot proved a strong supporter.

In 1962, when Elliot McAdam was eleven years old, his father Jimmy McAdam died at the age of seventy-five. Elliot's mother Dorcas died of cancer two years later. Before they died the McAdams had made arrangements for Elliot and his sister Faye to live with Amy McAdam, the wife of Jimmy's brother Tom, in Perth. Jimmy had purchased a house for Amy and Tom in Perth and given Amy lifetime residency after Tom died.

In Perth, Elliot boarded at Christchurch Grammar School, and his sister Faye at Perth Ladies' College. Young Elliot missed his Aboriginal family. Contact with them was not encouraged, although they wrote letters asking for him to go back to Darwin. With a year of school to go, Elliot saved some money from a summer job, borrowed the rest from a mate whose father used to own the Fitzroy Crossing pub, and ran away. In Darwin he worked as a trainee manager for Woolworths, then for Northern Territory Government Stores, and then took off for Newcastle Waters to visit his family, before staying with Charlie and Val in Alice Springs for nearly a year.

A series of jobs led to Adelaide and enrolment in the newly established Aboriginal Task Force. It was 1973, the year after the Tent Embassy. Elliot was politically aware, educated, articulate and determined, and for the next twenty years he worked for Aboriginal rights, starting as a field officer with the Aboriginal Legal Rights Movement (ALRM). In his time as Director of the Aboriginal Community Centre in Adelaide, the first Nunga radio show and child-care agencies were set up. With Gary Foley and John Tregenza he carried out a major review of Aboriginal health in South Australia in the '70s. As Director of the South Australian Aboriginal Health Organisation he was involved in setting up all the community-based health services in South Australia, at a time when the South Australian Health Commission was providing a service that was 'basically bandaids and Aspros. Health was the most pressing need at the time, and I consider that the best thing I've ever done.'

He was also a keen follower of Australian Rules Football. Elliot used to drive Greg to football practice. By the time Greg was sixteen he was playing for North Adelaide in the South Australian National Football League (SANFL). Elliot remembers his first league game.

'When he came on it was the last quarter and you could tell that he was going to be exceptional. It was a big thrill. He just had all the skills.' Greg continued to play for North Adelaide for the next five years, and twice was awarded Best and Fairest Player. He played for South Australia when South Australia beat Victoria in an interstate match for the first time in seventeen years. A proud Val and Charlie flew to Adelaide to watch him play. As Greg said, it all happened very quickly for him.

**Greg McAdam:** It was a pretty hectic schedule really, playing with the league squad at the age of fifteen. There was training three nights a week, plus a Saturday match game, plus Sunday mornings training again. The thing that really kept me going while I was away from my family was the fact that I was playing footy, and I was having a lot of success. The rewards were really great for me.

I think one of the reasons I was successful as a junior was the discipline that was instilled in me as a young lad, so that when I came to another world I just went with it. If we had to run ten kilometres on a Sunday you just did it. When we were hunting kangaroos in the bush we had to get that kangaroo to take it home and once you got it there was satisfaction. It's a similar thing playing footy, chasing a ball – you just have to do it.

When I finished playing footy in Adelaide in '83, about four or five of us were being chased by different clubs in Melbourne. In those early years I played football with Kernahan, Bradley, Platten – we were all together in the South Australian under 21 side. Geelong, North Melbourne, and South Melbourne showed interest, but in '84 I went back to Alice Springs for a year.

•

Greg met his wife Dolly Hampton in Adelaide when they were both seventeen.

**Greg McAdam:** We were together from then on. I don't

know how Dolly coped. When I was in Adelaide from the age of sixteen to twenty-two, I always wanted to be the best and it was really a selfish thing, a sort of closed mind-set. Then one minute I was a football star and the next minute I was entrenched back in the community at home, which was really different for Dolly because she grew up in an urban environment, in Port Augusta.

I didn't realise until I went back to Alice for a while that it was something special, coming to the city when I was so young and being able to play football. When I went home and looked around at what was happening I realised how terrible life can be for some Aboriginal people in Alice Springs, living in the creek and those things. I thought, We don't have to be like this. I felt that it was wrong that other people did not have the chance I had, that a lot of our people don't get out of our own environment and succeed in another environment. In '84 when I went home that was probably the biggest turning point in my life.

The high point of my footy career was winning the grand final in Alice Springs for Souths in 1984. Obviously playing State was pretty special, but it was a different feeling when I played at home with Souths. I was assistant coach, and we won the first grand final the club had won in twenty-something years. There were just so many brilliant footballers playing for that club that I can't understand why they didn't win more premierships. Aboriginal people have really special skills, but we really didn't understand what success was because people put shit on us so much.

In 1985 I was drafted by St Kilda, played ten games and injured my knee. I think the reason I went to Saints was to satisfy my own expectations, and other people's expectations, and in a way I suppose I was relieved not to have the burden of those expectations when I couldn't play professional football any more. When I left Alice as a kid I felt that there was an expectation to do well, but it was probably just the expectation to do the right thing. I remember Dad talking to me in the room on the day I flew to Adelaide, and all he said was, 'Look after yourself, don't get involved with drugs, don't get involved with any bad people, just be sensible and do the right thing.' But I felt there were expectations, probably my own.

Dad and Mum were never ones for shouting on the sidelines, they were never pushy parents. Oh, I remember Dad when I was playing in the B-grade in Alice – I was about twelve or thirteen – someone in the opposition team punched me in the back of the head when I went for a mark. Dad flew onto the oval and they had a bit of a rough-up, but it was because I was only a kid.

My parents instilled discipline into us, and respect for other people, and I think that goes back to the way they were brought up by the old people. I'm very grateful for that. Not that I haven't had a lot of problems with things in my life, though. I remember when I was growing up, the things that stuck in my mind about Halls Creek and about Alice Springs were that you had to be a big-time fighter, big-time drinker, and a womaniser to be a man in the Aboriginal community. It's wrong, and that's a wrong perception that I grew up with, but that's what I remembered of Alice Springs and Halls Creek. What a lot of bullshit.

I've been involved in working for Aboriginal people ever since I stopped playing footy – in sport, youth sport and recreation, education, the Commonwealth Employment Service. I'm proud of my work. It's good to have something to offer.

●

Gilbert McAdam first represented the Northern Territory when he was ten years old. He represented the Territory in football and soccer and captained the Northern Territory primary school cricket team for the next three years. Gilbert boarded in Adelaide from the age of fourteen, after the manager and coach of North Adelaide showed interest in his ability on a recruiting trip to Alice Springs. While attending Nailsworth High School he was picked in the South Australian under 16 schoolboys' side. At sixteen he left school, got a job detailing cars, moved into a flat and was recruited for the North Adelaide under 17 side. In the same year, 1985, he played for South Australia in the under 17 Teal Cup competition.

Elliot McAdam thought that young Gilbert's football was as remarkable for his dedication as his broad range of skills.

**Elliot McAdam:** He was always independent and dedicated. Gilbert could have played soccer for Australia if he had wanted to – he was good enough. I also think that Gilbert could have played at least Sheffield Shield cricket; in fact, all the boys could have, had they wanted to. Gilbert was an outstanding cricketer. He used to score centuries in Adelaide all the time.

●

But Gilbert got homesick. He went back to Alice Springs to play the remainder of the season there with Souths, the club Charlie follows, then straight to Darwin to play with the Waratahs for the Top End 1985–86 summer season. In Darwin he met his wife, Violet Mills. Claremont Football Club in Perth asked him to play in 1986, but 1987 saw him back in Adelaide.

**Charlie:** Val was in Adelaide by that time. The coach at Central Districts was Neil Kerley and the manager was Chris Grant. Gilbert walked in there with his boots round his shoulders and asked Chris Grant for a game. Grant said, 'Okay, young feller, I'll give you a game.'

**Gilbert McAdam:**   It was towards the end of the 1987 season. They had a trial game on the Friday night and afterwards Chris Grant said, 'I'll get back to you.' It was two weeks before I heard from them. I was just about to ring up West Adelaide when the phone rang. Apparently Neil Kerley thought I had a bit of promise because when he saw me play he said straight away to Chris Grant, 'Get me his clearance.'

•

Gilbert played seventy-five games for Central Districts between 1988 and 1990. The first year he was runner-up for the coveted Magarey Medal, the SANFL award for the best and fairest player in the league. In 1989 he won the Magarey Medal, becoming the first Aboriginal player to do so. Like its equivalent in Victoria, the Brownlow Medal, the vote-counting and presentation dinner for the Magarey Medal is broadcast live on television. League president Max Basheer, when he announced the winner, referred not only to Gilbert's fairness, but also his magic on the field.

**Charlie:**   What a great moment it was for the whole family. I was in Alice Springs at the time, listening to the count on the radio, and everybody in Alice Springs, all his friends and their parents, were very excited. All his mates were crying. Next morning blokes came over to my flat congratulating me just as if I'd won the thing. My brother-in-law and I jumped in a car and drove to Adelaide to congratulate him, and there were celebrations and carrying on – that was the proudest moment for us all. Gilbert was the first Aboriginal person to win the Magarey Medal. He's a terrific little footballer and I hope he just carries on as long as he wants to. He's one of the very successful lads that really made it, made the big time. I'm very proud of him.

**Val McAdam:**   We were sitting around in the house in

Elizabeth, all the family, watching television with a bottle of champagne ready in case he won, because we thought he might win, and all of a sudden the computer broke down, but we knew he'd won it by then. I sat there, I couldn't get up. I was crying like mad. Violet asked me to babysit, and I said, 'No I won't. I'm taking off.' And we just went straight down to the clubhouse. We were very, very emotional.

**Elliot McAdam:** When the announcement was made Gilbert just burst into tears, on live TV. I was sitting at home watching it, and I cried with him. We all went out to Central Districts clubhouse. I don't think Gilbert slept for about three days after that.

It wrenched you to bits. Those kids were brought up in hard times and leaving aside the football and all the other achievements, I think it's just a credit to Charlie and Val that they have all turned out to be such good human beings.

•

Some weeks later Gilbert heard that he had been drafted by St Kilda. He was doubly pleased to be selected by the club that had drafted Greg and looked forward to playing in the same team as West Australian footballer Nicky Winmar. After completing his contract with Central Districts he moved to Melbourne in 1991, and has played AFL football ever since.

Adrian's record also reads as a blueprint for a sporting career. He represented the Northern Territory in cricket, soccer, football and basketball during primary school, and in football during secondary school. He played in the Teal Cup in 1986 and 1987 and captained the Northern Territory side in 1988, the year that he was picked for the All Australian side. In 1988, aged sixteen, he played league for North Adelaide in the Escort Cup, now the Foundation Cup. The following year he played his first senior game in the SANFL, but, disappointed at only playing in the seconds, he finished the season in Alice Springs and then played a full season in Darwin. For the 1989–90 season he was back in Adelaide in the seconds, before he returned to Alice with a shoulder injury.

Football in the AFL is different to playing in Alice Springs.

**Adrian McAdam:**   The professionalism, the training – everything's different, because you've got to work a bit harder to get where you want to be. When we used to play back at home all the supporters used to sing out to me, because I used to kick a few goals. They'd sing out, 'Kick five goals and we'll buy you a beer after the game.' I used to go out trying to kick four or five goals a game. Now it's a team game. I get into a situation where I should be able to kick a goal but I'll handball it on to someone in the clear.

●

In 1992 Adrian was picked in a team to play against Port Adelaide in a promotional match.

**Adrian McAdam:**   There were a few scouts from the AFL there, because at the time Brett Chalmers and Nathan Buckley were playing for Port Adelaide and they were big headlines. I played a good game and Greg Miller, the general manager from North Melbourne, said he was pretty interested and to keep in touch. He knew who I was because of the Teal Cup and state schoolboy competitions. I always wanted to play for Norths because when I was young I always barracked for North Melbourne. We played for the Roos back at home and their colours were blue and white, so I always liked the colours and I've always been a Roo. From then onwards I just had to wait for the November draft, which was about three or four months away, a long time to wait. I wasn't quite sure whether they were going to draft me or not, but when the draft did come through, North Melbourne picked me up. I flew out from Alice Springs the next day. I was all packed and ready to go.

●

Adrian found his brothers' support invaluable when he moved to Melbourne. Although he admired several well-known league players – like Blight, Dennings, Dench, and Fairley, German and Larkins – it was Greg who had been his role model.

**Adrian McAdam:**   He started everything off, and that gave me confidence. Greg and Gilbert have been good support and given me good advice. We talk more about how the footy is going and how I'm coping and all that sort of stuff, which is good because I don't talk too much about it with other people. Greg and Gilbert both have the experience behind them and it's good to talk to them and get their advice, just what to expect and what not to and all the ups and downs of it. If you get dropped, if you don't get put up, if you have a bad one, it's good to have their advice.

The guys playing back at home taught me a fair bit. I think Aboriginal people just have some sort of gift. They can do a lot with the ball on the ground. They just know how to dodge and evade, and I think it's the way they think as well, just the way they read the play.

●

Adrian made a startling debut in the Australian Football league in a night game at the MCG against Richmond.

**Adrian McAdam:**   In the beginning I played four reserve games and I kicked a few goals, which helped me get a chance in a league game against Richmond, which I think was round four or round five. I had my first shot, which was my first kick of the game, from the fifty-metre line, and I missed that – wasn't too far – but then about two, three minutes later I was in the same position and I was on the run. I had a kick but I got pushed in the back so I had a set shot, which was my second shot, and that was my first goal. I kicked seven goals that night.

●

Adrian went on to be a leading goal-kicker in his first season. He holds the league record for the most goals kicked by a player in his first three games: twenty-three. By the end of his sixth game he had kicked thirty-eight goals, including nine goals in one match against Collingwood. It is a measure of the interest in football in Melbourne that when Adrian was the only North Melbourne player who managed to kick a football into a garbage bin at training, the television crews were there.

His career has not been without frustration and incident. In the early years it was studded with tribunal appearances and outbursts, which disappeared with the support of the close team spirit at North Melbourne. Several contemporaries were old team mates or opponents from Teal Cup days, including Wayne Carey, Jose Romero, Rob Harvey, Chris Nash, Andrew Krakouer, and Gordon Fode.

Val and Charlie watch their sons play whenever possible. When North Melbourne played St Kilda in 1993 and the two brothers opposed each other, Pamela and Elizabeth got up a petition to have the game screened in Alice Springs. Charlie maintains a low-key approach with his sons. On the morning that Adrian wore his new grey trousers and Norths blazer for the first time, he walked into the living-room and said, 'Well, I'm off now, Dad.' Charlie looked up from his newspaper, glasses perched on the end of his nose. 'Play well, son,' was all he said. Val was a little more direct. 'Tell him

to lead out more,' she instructed long-distance from Adelaide.
Val enjoys the atmosphere at North Melbourne.

**Val McAdam:**   North Melbourne is a very friendly club. I
like Wayne Carey. When I met him he said to me, 'Should I call
you Mrs McAdam or Val?' I said, 'You can call me Mum or
Val. Everyone else does.'

●

For many Aboriginal sportsmen and women, sporting
achievement has been a tough battle against poverty and prejudice. When Adrian played in the 1993 North Melbourne
versus Richmond match, the media seized on the newcomer
from Alice Springs. One journalist tried to focus on the
romantic aspects of the Aboriginal lad who learned to kick a
football in a dusty backyard. Charlie was incensed. 'I had the
best-kept yard in Alice Springs,' he grumbled as he pasted the
clipping into a bulging scrapbook.

None of the McAdam children experienced the conflict
that Charlie had, and none experienced racism growing up in
Alice Springs. Charlie did not let his experiences affect his
children's upbringing. In fact he did not tell them about
Moola Bulla and Beagle Bay when they were growing up at
all. Val's attitude is matter-of-fact. 'You've just got to get out and
mix.' Their sons and daughters mirror this.

**Pamela (McAdam) Reilly:**   Dad was really strict when we
were going out with boys, but he never used to say things
like, Don't go out with a white bloke, or anything like that. We
used to go out with anybody and we still do. We had white
friends and black friends. We probably met most of our white
friends playing sport. I've never experienced any racist comments
to this day. But when I was at business college in Adelaide
and I used to go to football to watch Gregory and Gilbert,

you'd hear people saying 'black so-and-so'. There was one occasion where Gilbert was playing for Central Districts. Mum and I were sitting up at the fence and people started calling Gilbert 'black so-and-so'. Mum turned around and she had her say and it was just so funny. She told them what to do and where to go.

**Greg McAdam:** I experienced racism for the first time when I was playing football. I found it really funny, because people who were trying to put me down with racist comments couldn't identify what nationality I was because I had light skin and an Afro hairstyle. People really didn't know whether to call me wog or black.

A lot of people used to come down from Alice Springs to Adelaide to watch me play – Mum and Dad, friends and family – and I did notice that if I was with a group of Aboriginal friends or family, racism wasn't really directed at me but it was directed at people who were with me. 'You're okay but he's not okay' was the attitude. How can people say that, when that other person next to me could be my first cousin or my uncle or someone? That's the sort of racism I experienced a hell of a lot, and I still do experience that sort of racism. At a meeting, for example, people will be talking about Aboriginal people in a really derogatory manner because they don't realise that I am Aboriginal.

**Adrian McAdam:** I never think about the politics of being an Aboriginal footballer when I'm playing. I just concentrate on my footy, and I'm pretty sure everybody else does too, because if you put other things on your mind you don't perform. That's definitely one thing you don't want to worry about. I've copped a few comments – particularly in the first year when I was playing in the reserves, because the other guys want to make it up in the league too, and probably calling someone names is the easiest way to put someone off their game. I found it pretty hard to cope with at first, but when I got up in to the seniors you can't really hear many comments because of the crowd, plus you're concentrating more as well. It didn't worry me too much.

●

For Gilbert McAdam, the game that stands out in his career was a St Kilda versus Collingwood match in 1993.

**Gilbert McAdam:**   I had three great years at St Kilda. They treated us really well and I made a lot of friends. I was also lucky enough to play in the finals rounds, which is the pinnacle really. But the game I'll never forget was that game against Collingwood.

We always had really good battles against Collingwood. That day at half-time in the reserves match, the league players went out to check the condition of the oval, like we always do. I was walking around with Nicky [Winmar] and all the Collingwood supporters started abusing us, calling us petrol sniffers, abos, coons – they were just calling us everything. I said to Nicky, 'Oh well, you'd better get Best on Ground today, mate. We don't have to put up with that.' But then I got Best on Ground and Nicky was runner-up, so that was really good. They thought they were going to put us off our game, but we were really pumped up. It was even more rewarding to beat Collingwood on their home ground. I reckon in the three years I was playing for St Kilda we played Collingwood six or seven times and we would have won more than we lost – including the fights. *(laughs)*

●

As the victorious St Kilda team was walking off the Collingwood ground, Nicky Winmar turned to the crowd and pulled up his football jumper to point triumphantly at his brown skin. In response to allegations of racism in football, the AFL organised a match in Darwin in January 1994 between the Collingwood side and the Aboriginal All Stars, a team composed of Aboriginal players from different league teams across Australia. Gilbert McAdam, apart from playing in the match, was also one of its organisers. Adrian McAdam and Nicky Winmar were absent from the All Stars team: St Kilda refused Winmar's appearance, and Adrian chose not to risk jeopardising his team's chances in the Foster's Cup.

At the end of the 1993 season the AFL sent Gilbert to Darwin to promote Australian Rules Football among schoolchildren. His work included a four-day trip to Halls Creek.

**Gilbert McAdam:**   That was the first time I had been to Halls Creek since I was a kid, so I had not seen that mob for about twelve years. I think it must have hit me a bit. Everyone was crying for me. They knew me when I was a little kid but they'd only seen me on television since then. I just saw my people, what sort of conditions they were living in and what they had going for them, compared to what I'd been doing for the last ten years.

I was lucky. At least I had Dad mob to send me to school, whereas some of these poor people – it just made me feel sad for them. Some of those poor things are my own flesh and blood, and when you're Aboriginal it's a very strong connection, it's just like it's happening to you. It freaked me out.

When I got back to Melbourne I was out of contract with St Kilda and there were problems renegotiating my contract. I did two weeks' training with them, but in the end I was thinking about giving up football altogether.

●

Gilbert's response to his dilemma was to go home again. He threw his gear into the back of his Toyota at the end of training,

194

BOUNDARY LINES

and headed north with his three-year-old son, young Charlie, beside him. They drove to Alice Springs, then to Tennant Creek, where he and Elliot talked through the night, and on to Halls Creek to sit down with his family for a while and think things through.

When he returned he accepted a contract with Brisbane, and went on to play the 1994 season with the Bears.

**Gilbert McAdam:**   In retrospect that was the best thing I've ever done. Violet and I and the kids are going back to Halls Creek as much as we can now. Violet loves it up there.

We go and stay with the family and they show us all the things about our culture that we want to learn. Aunty Mutta, a little tiny lady, she teaches language in the schools and she's going though all the different words with me.

The women showed Violet which tree to get honey from, and they showed us how to make a coolamon. Those coolamons, they look pretty simple, but even after I cut down the right tree and cut it out roughly it must have taken us six or seven hours, even though we had a tomahawk. In the old days all they had was a little stone. You gotta be real patient and chip away. You can't chip too deep because you'll go too far and there'll be a hole in it.

Yunguntji told me some of the stories. I've got them all on tape. That Moon feller, he was a real larrikin. But the thing is, if you sat down with those old people for the rest of your life, you still wouldn't know half of what they know.

The most amazing thing about all this is that Dad didn't tell us anything about it. He was at Beagle Bay, but the first I ever heard of Beagle Bay was when I was studying at Monash University in 1993. I suppose he just wanted us to have a fresh start, but now everyone is old enough to understand it.

# Springvale to Halls Creek: Gilbert's Story

DORIS FLETCHER DESCRIBED Charlie's brother Gilbert as 'a short man, and a hard-working man'. Gilbert has the bushman's quiet smile, and the rolling walk of someone who has spent a large part of his life in the saddle. His approach to things, including the setting down of this account, is precise. Gilbert's wife Evelyn is the daughter of Jack and Mona Green, who is an author and matriarch of the Jaru people. They have been married for twenty-six years and have six children.

**Gilbert McAdam Senior:**   When my father sold Springvale my mother and I went along with it, more or less like a cow and calf.

I heard a story from the old people that my mother had a little half-caste boy before me. In those days the police were coming around to pick up all those half-caste kids, and they got terrified when they heard the police were coming because they thought they were going to kill the baby, so they turned around and killed it. A couple of years later I came along and one old woman here called Buttercup, she took me away until things settled down.

I must have been about three years old when Quiltys bought the property. They saw me down at the Aboriginal camp, in those days it was called, and because I was half-caste they reckoned they will get this little feller and grow him up. They had another little full-blood they brought over here from Coolibah Station in Queensland, a year older than me. They called him Finnigan Quilty. I think they must have got me for a mate for him.

I was a bit lost at first. They had a high fence around the garden and I remember us looking down the camp to my mother all the time, trying to go back. I used to run to my mother when she came into work, wanting to suck. Then I got used to the Quilty ways, because we all used to sit around the same table to eat, and in the end I sort of stayed there.

The Quiltys had eight little Aboriginal kids there, besides myself: Clancy, Russia Clifton – Clancy and Russia were brothers – Rammel Peters and his younger brother; Yunguntji's daughters Matilda and Judy – Sally they call her now – Finnigan Quilty and Lorna Thomas.

When I was about four or five I can remember doing jobs around the house, carting sand for the garden from the creek with a little trolley. As soon as they were strong enough the girls worked in the house and the boys went out mustering. We used to get one shirt and trousers, no boots. Our legs were too short to reach the stirrups, so old Tom Quilty cut the toes off his old leather slippers and tied them onto the saddle, like clogs for us to put our feet in. We had the same clothes out in the stockcamp for, it must have been, four weeks at a time.

One year when I was only seven or eight the mob from Moola Bulla came up to tend the Springvale muster, to get their cattle back, any that were mixed up with ours. In those days kids couldn't get the right size trousers to fit. I had baggy trousers on and I was holding them up with one hand, and I had the bridle in the other hand trying to catch this bloomin' horse. I couldn't catch him because I needed one hand to hold onto my trousers, and every time the horse saw the bridle he took off.

Old Tom Quilty sang out, 'Take your trousers off!'

I said, 'What?'

'Take your trousers off!'

I was really embarrassed. I had to pull my trousers off so I could put the bridle on the horse and I had to ride all that afternoon with no trousers on.

In the stockcamp we kids used to have just corned beef and damper, but no tea. We weren't allowed to drink tea because the old boss reckoned it wasn't good for your nerves. We used to have tea in the homestead, but we weren't allowed to have tea out in the stockcamp, so we used to ask the old people for tea. We were all related of course. Our job, the kids', was to go down to the soak they dug in the creek, to fill the billy cans up with water ready for breakfast, and when we picked up the billies from the old people they used to leave a bit of tea in it and we used to go down the soak and have a drink. The only thing was, it used to taste a bit funny because of the saccharine they used in the stockcamp. They carried saccharine, not sugar, because it was less weight for the packhorses. So we used to have our cuppa tea, fill all the billies up and take them back ready for the morning.

Half the time we were hungry. We knew where all the bush food was but Tom Quilty would never let us get off the horse to get any. We used to work our way around it. We'd be driving a mob of cattle along. Every time we'd go past a bush plum someone would drift out, chase some calf around one side of the bush, and all of a sudden drop your hat off so you could get off and rake up all these little dried plums – taluni – just put them in your pocket, dust and leaf and all, and start pickin' them out of your pocket as you rode along. Same thing with bush watermelon. This old bloke would keep an eye on us all the time, so if you saw a bush watermelon, you'd ride past, drop the hat off and get a mouthful, jam as much as you can into your mouth and keep riding. Tom Quilty was tough on us, but he was straight and fair. I don't think it did me much harm. I suppose it was part of life.

As I grew older we used to do schoolwork in the lunch hour, from twelve to two, in the stockcamp. We used to stand up and say our times-tables up to twelve, Finnigan, Rammel and me. We'd all be mucking around, laughing at each other, but we used to say our times-tables and do a bit of writing. When it was two o'clock we'd go back to work again.

It was probably when Rod Quilty took over Lansdowne that we went mustering there during the wet, to give him a hand. I only remember parts of it, when something really good or really bad happened. That's how it was, because we were only young and we were working fairly hard. Charlie mob [Charlie and the other ringers] took all the horses across and me and old Tom took all the dogs. My job was to look after the dogs, so I went over in the little two-wheel trailer with all the dogs hooked on behind the jeep. I had to tie the dogs up and feed them. We used to let them out when we yarded up wild cattle, because when you let the dogs out the calves run straight back to their mother, or if there was a big bull they used to cling to the bull's nose and pull him down. We had six or seven dogs, mainly crosses between a boxer and a bulldog. They were all pretty colours, red ones, and red and white ones, and really good cattle dogs.

One part of the muster, we were going along at night behind a mob of cattle. We started during the day, but we just couldn't make it before dark and we ended up going into the night. It was raining and dark. I kept asking one of the Aboriginal stockmen, 'How far is the camp?'

'Oh, just over the ridge.'

'How far now?'

'Oh, just over the ridge.'

That seemed the longest ridge. I was only six or seven years old at the time, and I was pretty tired.

After we came back from Lansdowne we had to go and check the fence out in what used to be the Six Mile horse paddock. Clancy, Finnigan and I were with Tom Quilty out there when the jeep broke down. We had trouble starting it. Tom told me to feel the spark plug to see if there was power coming through while he was touching the starter. There was power all right. I got a shock.

'How's she goin' there mate, Gilbo?'

'Bit of a spark,' I said. That was an understatement.

'How's the next one?'

I got a bit of grass on that one. 'Oh, she's right boss.'

'Keep goin'.' He couldn't see the grass because he had the bonnet up.

'She's right, Boss!' I didn't want to argue with the boss. We still had to walk back home from there.

The worst part of the muster would be when we kids went on what they call the dog watch, the time of day when you start the cattle feeding where they are going to camp. It starts late afternoon and finishes about six or seven o'clock. You tail the cattle around and start putting them on the camp, while the men are having their tea before they start the main shift watching the bullocks. Some of the kids were that tired we'd fall asleep on top of the horse. The old horse would head back to the camp and we'd look up nearly at the camp and see the campfire – 'Uh-oh' – we'd turn around quick. Tom Quilty used to make us sing on the dog watch to settle the cattle down, and so you could tell where the next bloke was when you were riding around. He could always hear if we fell asleep. He'd come up behind you and yell out, 'Sing, you bugger!'

You always had one eye on Tom Quilty when you were mustering. One time after dinner I was riding alongside the wing of the mob, half asleep too, sort of daydreaming. I heard a little rattle behind me. I looked back and Tom Quilty's coming at full speed with the whip. He got me all right, but when I sneaked another look back he's under the horse with one leg up. The girth had slipped. I thought, Oh, this is it, he is gonna kill me now. Funny thing, when we got back to camp, he never said a word.

Another time we were droving through Bedford Downs and three of us kids were skiting among ourselves about who was the best rider. There was me, Norman Echo and Finnigan, I think. We didn't hear Mick Quilty come up behind us until he said, 'Bullshit.' That's all he said. Mick was six or seven years older than us.

After we delivered the cattle on that muster we went back to Springvale. There were new little saddles with a proper little bucket for your foot waiting at the station. We saw them there and we were real proud. We were so happy, each kid picking out the one he liked. 'Oh, this my saddle.' 'This my saddle.' Sure enough, they were for us.

We changed plant for another muster then, so we got fresh horses. I think Mick probably reckoned, These young fellers, I'll give them something that'll buck. It was after Charlie had left and I got this chestnut mare called Molly that he'd been riding. We started mustering again around Whitewater and we stopped at Yarring – the yards on Springvale Hill – for dinner camp. We were rarin' to try these little saddles out. After dinner I jumped on this chestnut mare with the little pad and she threw me straight up. Bang. I got back on. She threw me again. Albert – he was a good rider, that bloke – he came up to me and he said 'See that thing [the monkey strap], you hang onto that thing real tight and you watch her head.' But she threw me again. I just couldn't ride her for some reason. The third time, I blacked out and I couldn't hear anything for a while. Mick Quilty said to Albert, 'You'd better ride this mare for him.' I wasn't the only one that came off that day. When the horses were fresh there would be blokes flying everywhere.

When we grew out of the little pads we got bigger saddles with proper knee-pads on them, and proper riding boots. As we grew older we were given more responsibility, and we were left alone tailing the cattle. When you were tailing cattle you got bored. We had to do something, so we used to get a stick and write our name on the knee-pad or draw something, a tree or a horse.

At the end of the mustering season we handed our saddles in to be repaired. Tom Quilty used to do all the repairs himself. Next year, when we got the saddles back at the start of the mustering season, old Tom Quilty had cut the knee-pads off.

'What's that for?'

'For scribbling your name on it.'

They looked funny, those saddles with no knee-pads. It made us aware of being in balance with the horse, because we had no knee-pads to hang onto stopping and turning. We had to use our feet properly then.

●

Rammel Peters was one of the children taken from the camp to live with Gilbo and the others in the homestead.

**Rammel Peters:**    Quilty was a pretty tough old feller. Everything we were supposed to do. We used to do school, and work, and mustering. After school we used to mop floor, wash plates, cook bread and everything. Only playtime was when we used to go down the creek on Saturday or Sunday.

He used to line up all the bunks there in the homestead.

Night-time he used to come out and look at us, make sure that we sleep. Sometimes we used to whisper and he'd come out and say (*gruffly*), 'Go ter sleep!'

He was watching us all the time, evey time. He always used to watch us. Very tough. He used to give us a hidin' with the stockwhip. But he used to love kids, Quilty, he loved kids. He used to get cranky when we done somethin' wrong, we used to get a hidin', but when we used to do the right thing, work and that, then he loved us.

Fun times? Only fun time I remember was Christmas. Oh, and race time – that was when they used to go into town to the racecourse and leave us alone. But Christmas time was big fun, that time. They used to have foot race, bag race, spear throwin'. One mob, big mob that side, other mob this side – tug o' war, that's it. For the races all the kids got prizes – balloon, lolly, saddle gear, glass, shaving gear, everything. Special feed, one woman there used to cook it.

We used to swap. One Christmas all the Bedford Downs mob and Lansdowne mob come to Springvale, and we used to meet up there, big fun there and then go back. Next time we all go over to Bedford Downs.

Beginning of the wet he used to take us away. We didn't know what he was doin' and then we were poddy-dodgin'. (*laughs*) We used to draft out the cleanskins. Some of us work the calves on that side, other mob keep the cows on this side, so the cows forget their kid – I thought it was cruel.

In the stockcamp, only time you have a bit of a blow is when you wash your clothes or saddlecloth. But I used to like workin' with cattle and horses. Cattlework was just like fun, riding a horse, chasin' scrubbers, chasin' bulls, muckin' around together. We had a good life on the station. Even though we had no wage, life was pretty good.

**Gilbert McAdam Senior:** By the time I was fourteen the

country was opening up. Somehow the welfare system started coming in, and they must have approached the Quiltys and asked them why I was not going to school. The Quiltys decided to send me to Perth. I'd been working in the stockcamp for about eight years by the time I went to school. I could break in a horse and do just about anything on the station. I thought the plane trip to Perth was really good. Maybe that was when I decided I'd fly one day.

Anyway, I went to school, to Clontarf Boys Home. I got into that many fights, with the other white kids calling me 'boong', but I got used to taking it. In the end I thought, Ah, what's the use.

Two years I went to school, coming back home in the holidays. That was it. One day at school they asked me, 'How old are you?' At that time I was in the footy team and they wanted to see my birth certificate. I only woke up then to the way age is important to white people. I had to write to Mrs Quilty now, my foster mother. She sent me a letter and she gave me her father's birthday, 1st of October, for 1945. They reckoned I was about three years old when they bought that station in 1948. So they gave me that birthday, and I suppose I'm stuck with it now.

When I came back, her son Mick Quilty was running the camp on Springvale. I spent one year out in the stockcamp with him, and I had the urge to go back and do a mechanic course for some reason – I think I wanted to go back and play football. I had everything booked to go back to Perth when the Quiltys asked me to stay, and Mick ended up getting married and moving to a property called Ruby Plains. So we had no head stockman from August for that year, I think it was '64.

We kept asking them, 'Who's gonna be the head stockman?' They got a white bloke and it was completely different to the way we were taught. We kids grew up together and we knew only one way of doing the job. When this white bloke turned up he seemed to do everything wrong. Tom Quilty ended up sackin' him because he didn't carry out his duties.

Basil Quilty had more or less taken over by that stage, because Tom was getting pretty old. Basil was living on Bedford, still with Lou Lou in those days. He took me on a trial muster for three weeks, although I didn't know that at the time. He must have been satisfied with the way I performed because at the end of the three weeks he said to me, 'Well, you'll have to be head stockman.' I was nineteen years old. All my life I wanted one thing, to be head stockman on Springvale. Even as a kid it was my little dream. But the first two years were the hardest part of my life. I had all these mates, we used to play together and I was something above them now, couldn't sit with them to eat or anything. I didn't feel that way because I grew up with them. They were all full-bloods, and being half-caste I found it harder. All our mothers were related.

There were some funny things that happened. One time we were mustering there alongside a creek and a cleanskin micky with big horns, half-Brahman, was heading for the creek. I reckoned I'd get him before he crossed the creek, so I took off and turned him and jumped off the horse. I was running downhill to grab him and throw him when this thing turned around, and all I could do was grab him by the horns. I thought, This is it, I'm gone, because they usually jerk their head up and I would have gone flying if he had. But for some reason this bull started to back off, and another feller jumped off and grabbed him by the tail and threw him. It was close.

That year I went for a bit of a holiday over to Alice Springs to see my brother Charlie. It was the first time I had seen him since he left. To tell you the truth, I don't know how I knew he was there. The following year, '66, we both competed in the Alice Springs Rodeo. We went in the second division bronc ride first, but didn't do any good. Then there was the first divi-

sion, the Australasian Champion Bronc Ride, with all the top
riders. I went over and I said, 'Look I've come all the way
from WA to ride,' and one old bloke let me enter. I suppose he
didn't know I had already been in the second division. And I
won it. First one in my life. I couldn't believe it. It was a bit of a
boost to my confidence. I couldn't wait to get back home and
show this mob the ribbon.

For the next twenty-five years I competed in rodeos,
mainly at Negri in the Territory, Kununurra, Fitzroy, Derby
and Halls Creek in the Kimberley. I won the saddle bronc ride at
all those places – that's one of the main events in roughriding. I
gave it up a couple of years ago, but I still have a go at the roping
and bulldogging. I miss the bronc riding, it's like a sport to me.
People say I'm too old, but if you've been sitting on a horse since
you were old enough to stand up, who are they to say?

It must have been thirteen years I ran the camp on Springvale.
In '68 Evelyn and I got married. Now I had a wife and a little
daughter, but we were still living in the big open quarters
with the other workers when a mechanic turned up from
Perth. Basil Quilty had taken over the running of both stations because by that time old Tom was in a wheelchair. The
mechanic came along and they built him a house, a nice little
cottage. I was scratchin' my head. Anyhow, I had to say something to Basil Quilty.

One day I said to him, 'How come this bloke can get a
house, yet he's just come up from Perth, and I've been here all
my life?'

'Oh,' he said, 'he's a qualified mechanic, we've got to do
that for him.'

I told Basil I was going to Alice Springs, and he said, 'Oh no,
don't leave. We'll build you a house.' They ended up building a
two-bedroom house and I was the happiest man.

Any work there was to do, I used to really get into it. I
thought, This is good, I'm goin' to live in my own house,

have some privacy now I'm married.' We planted fruit trees and made a real home there.

One evening while we were living in that cottage I heard the sound of the curlew calling close by. I looked out the window and it was right there on the lawn, and I knew my mother had died, because when the curlew comes up close to you it's bringing bad news, usually of a death. That's what we believe. That willy wagtail, jikirrji, he's another dangerous little bird. The old people used to tell us to watch out for him, and when we were little kids if we saw a willy wagtail we used to go racing back to the camp. When I got older I saw a picture of a magician all dressed up in a black suit and white shirt, and I thought it was funny that the katiya dress up magicians like the willy wagtail, because they play tricks too.

Things went on at Springvale for a little while, until there was a slump in meat prices and Basil asked me to go over to Bedford Downs. They didn't want to employ another head stockman and Basil wanted me to muster the two properties. Springvale was 500 000 acres. Bedford was a million and a half.

When they said we had to shift over to Bedford I felt, Oh well, they're the boss and it's a challenge. Plus I thought I was part of the family and I'd help them out for a few years and then go back to Springvale to live.

All the kids were there, Stephen and Kenny, Lou Lou's kids, giving me a hand to pack up. We started carting all the gear out, and I hung on till I got to the last bit of gear I had to pull out of the house, and I had to bust out cryin' in front of all those kids. At that little house we had mangoes and all sorts of citrus fruit growing, and they were all starting to have fruit. All the grapes we planted were comin' up. Our little cottage is still there on Springvale. Funny thing was, we went to Bedford and we started to do the same thing there, growing things, and one woman said to me, 'I wouldn't bother growing fruit trees.' I had a sense then there was something going on.

For the next four years I had eighteen men working under me, doing the cattlework. We had a gyrocopter those days, for mustering. We used to muster from morning to night. Some would be branding flat out while others were mustering. We hung in there.

Towards a bit of a break there one time, we took a big mob of cattle across to Springvale ready to send them to the meatworks. We counted out two road trains into one yard, ready for trucking the next day, and the rest in the other yard. We had to camp by the yard with our night horses, in case the cattle rushed. Finnigan, Norman Echo and I were sleeping camped there and it started to rain. I got up and all our horses were gone. They must have pulled away. I said to my two mates, 'Bugger this, I'll have to walk back. What happens if cattle rush, we can't do anything anyway. No horses.'

So I started walking and I fell asleep on my feet walking along, I suppose exhausted from the pressure of work. The lightning and thunder woke me up in the middle of the hill. I was heading bush. I was lucky that I knew that country. I looked around and waited for lightning to flash and then I could see a bit of a hill and a snappy gum tree. I was thinking back, trying to place it, because I know Springvale so well, and finally I worked out where that hill and snappy gum were, knew that there was a bloodwood here, and a coolibah there, and I knew where I was. So I backtracked, which wasn't easy because it was pitch dark, until I heard that low sound of bullocks in the yards and I walked over to them.

We mustered flat out for four years, and meanwhile they got another manager for Springvale. I had a funny feeling they were going to sell out. Old Tom Quilty and Olive shifted to Bunbury and I felt half lost, because to me that bloke was really good. As a kid I was his offsider. He took me everywhere with him. It was as if he was grooming me for responsibility later on. When we kids used to tend the muster, Tom would put me in charge of the other little kids. When he went to buy properties, we flew to Inverway and Ruby Plain and Tom took me as his main gate-opener. I sort of half missed him. I had sensed for a while there was something wrong. A couple of times I wanted to leave and Mrs Quilty said, 'Oh no, don't leave, because you'll benefit when the old feller dies.' I couldn't work out what she meant by that. When Tom went to Bunbury I felt that I had done my bit for the family.

It had taken me years to realise I had to go and start on my own. Looking back, I knew there was something wrong, that the Quiltys were going to sell Springvale and Bedford Downs, from the time we had to move from Springvale to Bedford. In my own quiet time I must have cried for about a week, at leaving. All I ever wanted was to live on Springvale. It's hard when people tell you what to do all your life, and all of a sudden you find you're let go into a new world. I had to make my own decisions, and I knew I had to make the right ones.

●

In the 1960s the saddler and businessman R.M. Williams instigated the Tom Quilty Gold Cup, an annual 24-hour endurance ride to 'keep alive the spirit of the pioneering horsemen'. Quilty donated a solid-gold cup as first prize.

Tom Quilty was awarded the Order of the British Empire in 1973 for his services to the cattle industry. In the same year his book of poetry *The Drover's Cook* was published in aid of the Flying Doctor Service. Quilty died in 1979 at the age of ninety-three.

The Kija people began to leave Springvale years before Gilbert and his family left. When Rusty and Rammel Peters' father was killed in a fall at Rosie's Yard, not long after Charlie left Springvale to go droving, the family left Springvale and moved from station to station in the East Kimberley. Yunguntji took his family to Alice Downs, and then other stations. In the '60s and '70s it became increasingly difficult for Aboriginal stockmen to find work. The payment of award wages filtered into the Kimberley. Road trains replaced droving teams, stations were fenced, and aerial mustering further eroded the reliance on Aboriginal labour. Stations were passing from families to corporate control. The slump in meat prices which precipitated Gilbert's move from Springvale compounded the situation.

Along with a number of other families, the Peters finally moved to a small area of crown land at Turkey Creek, which officially became Warmun Community in 1975.

**Rammel Peters:**   Before that we were living on the stations: Mabel Downs, Lissadell, Alice Downs, Texas. When the award wages came, the manager said, 'Oh, I can't have that many blokes.' So that was when we left. They told us, 'You'll get unemployment [benefit].'

We didn't know what unemployment was. We didn't know that job! Thought it was like yardbuilding, fencing maybe, another job. *(laughs)* We didn't know it was sit-down money. We didn't know what to do.

•

Rammel Peters is now Chairperson of Warmun Community. His older brother Rusty, Charlie's jimari, is now an artist living and working in Kununurra. In his paintings broad areas of muted red, ochres and blacks, with shapes delineated in white dots, map the country of the Kija people and its stories. His work has been widely exhibited. He says that he does not miss the life on the stations.

For many Aboriginal people in the Kimberley the exodus from the stations was accompanied by their first encounters with a cash economy and alcohol, and the majority weathered what was effectively a second dispossession. The casualties of this sudden change were seen by many non-Aboriginal people as justification for their paternalism.

Gilbert McAdam Senior made the painful decision to leave Bedford Downs of his own accord in 1980. He set out to establish his own contract mustering business, for which, having been Quilty's head stockman for seventeen years, he was well qualified. But by this time he faced stiff competition in the changed cattle industry. Sometimes his efforts were blocked by prejudice, which was not always restricted to his working life.

A quietly indignant Evelyn McAdam described one incident when the family was returning from a visit to some of her family in Queensland. On the way through Alice Springs one evening they stopped to buy groceries. Evelyn sat in the car with baby Kym and the other four children while Gilbert went into the shop. She saw two policemen watching Gilbert. They came over to the car and leaned in the window.

**Evelyn McAdam:**   They kept asking me, 'How much has he had to drink? He's been drinking, hasn't he?' They kept trying to get me to say that Gilbert had been drinking. We camped on the road the night before, so we might have looked a bit untidy, but that was no excuse for the way they were carrying on. In the end they got sick of it and they went away.

●

The irony was not lost on Gilbert, who drinks beer occasionally and sparingly, and Evelyn, a devout Christian who does not drink at all.

For the most part, incidents of prejudice were more subtle: a chance comment, a contract cut short, different treatment from whitefellers.

**Gilbert McAdam Senior:**   I've found good friends among

katiya, blackfellers and yellerfellers. There's good and bad in everyone, but I still feel that Aboriginal people are judged as a group, and judged wrongly.

When I left Bedford there was a contract going at Ord River for a mustering team, and there was a property called Koongee Park for sale as well at the time. The manager at Ord River offered me a five-year mustering contract, but he said I had to build a steel yard first. I thought it was worth it for a five-year contract, and there was so much mustering with the number of cattle on that place I was thinking I could save up and buy myself a little property and run some cattle.

Just when I finished building the yard the manager came over and said, 'What are your kids doing pickin' on my boy?' There was some disagreement between my daughter Deborah and the manager's son while they were playing. I thought he was unreasonable, but I'd done too much work to walk away just from some kid trouble.

We ended up signing that contract for that muster. I had a Toyota, and that was another story. We went up to Darwin to buy it. When I walked into the Toyota showroom the salesman just looked at me. He asked me what I wanted. I explained and he said, 'Oh, sorry we haven't got any of those.' I knew they had but I wasn't going to say anything, just said, 'Okay,' and went to walk out.

The salesman called after me. 'How were you going to pay for that vehicle?'

'Cash,' I said. I had the money in the bank.

'Oh,' he said, 'we might have something. Come and have a cup of tea, mate, and we'll see what we can do.' He was really friendly after that.

Anyway, I had that Toyota. I bought a demountable yard, and Evelyn's father gave me some horses and saddles. We walked 'em across from Osmond Valley Station past the Bungle Bungles, through Bulmah to Ord River Station, and started mustering on horseback. I knew who all the best stockmen were, so I had four really good blokes working for me. We did all right, just horseback mustering. Our first pay I thought, This is good.

We had a contract for a particular area on Mistake Creek, but another mob of contract musterers from the Territory started coming across our boundary. We mustered one side, trying to hunt all the cattle across, and this mob used to fly over in the early morning with the aeroplane. Soon as they'd see the campfire they'd dip the wings. I didn't want to stir any more trouble. You sort of learn to keep quiet. But they got their cut out of it. I reckon they took most of the cattle.

That went on for a year. Toward the end of the year I bought myself a truck, thinking I'd build up slowly. I was putting money away too, so I could pay my wages bill. I thought if I didn't come out on top, at least I wouldn't owe anybody any money. At Christmas time I paid all my men off and I gave a bonus to two blokes who stuck to me right through. That was the way we worked. I respected them and I think they respected me.

I thought I had five years and I was building up slowly. I must have had, oh, $50 000 saved up now, for this property – a good start, I thought. At the end of that year I went to see an accountant in Derby. I walked in and showed him all the accounts and things, and he said, 'Goodness. Very strange for a black man to earn that much money.'

The funny thing was that he was a Christian bloke, and I went to him because I thought a Christian would be more understanding. Then I got hit with provisional tax. I didn't know anything about paying provisional tax, and the accountant had not told me about it. I only had $10 000 left after I paid provisional tax.

Next year I was getting ready for the mustering season again. I had just put a crate on the truck when they told me I couldn't have the contract. The manager gave the contract to some mates of his. Ord River Station was run by the Department of Agriculture so I had to ring a bloke in the office of the minister in Perth. I explained that I'd bought all this gear and was ready to give it a good go. I thought I had the contract for five years, and after all the work I had done there, yard building and putting in electric fences to hold the cattle, I thought they should consider at least two or three years.

He told me my price was too high, so I dropped my price and they gave me the contract for the second year. I was floating. I got all the gear together, horses and everything, and all the men wanted to work with me again. I thought, Well, I'm on my way now.

They told me to muster the same area as the year before, so there weren't nearly as many cattle there. The other mob who had the contract to muster the rest of the place got straight in a helicopter, and you should have seen the cattle they got – load after load they trucked out of their section. We were just battling, while they had the best part of the country to muster, and twice as much of it. One problem was that we had to cross the Ord River all the time. It was harder to muster across the river, especially when the cattle had been mustered before. The bank is steep and there might be one or two pads for them to go down, so the cattle start doubling back when they hit a certain point because they know, they've been mustered there before. Trucks taking the cattle out were gettin' stuck, and we'd be there in the middle of the night getting them out. The other mob had the western side of the river so the trucks didn't have to cross the river.

It was all right, I was getting a bit of money in and we kept goin', but we got nothing like the numbers they did with the chopper. To rub salt into the wound, the other contractors made good use of the yards, all the facilities I had developed. At the end of the year I went contract fencing all around the area, and that year I just broke even.

At that time I realised that choppers were the way to go with mustering. I applied to DEET [Department of Employment, Education and Training] for a training grant to get a fixed-wing pilot licence, but they refused because they said I had to have Year 12 education. I went ahead and got my fixed-wing licence in Darwin with my own money. That was a magic feeling. After that DEET agreed to fund a training grant for the chopper licence.

I went to Perth for part of the helicopter licence course. There were a lot of people from Singapore and the small islands there to do navigation courses – because Australia's so wide it's ideal for nav. Even there, there was racial abuse. I was getting rubbished by people there who were blacker than me!

I was that used to it I just plugged away. I had my set goal. In the end I got my chopper licence. It took me seven months of study. I did all the commercial exams but I failed those by one subject, the met [meteorological], the first and easiest exam from the fixed-wing licence, so I was going to go back again to finish it.

Meanwhile I was appointed pastoral advisor for the Billiluna and Lake Gregory communities. The mob at Lake Gregory, or Malan they call it, got some of their land back there. Evelyn and the kids and I moved down to Billiluna, on the edge of the Great Sandy Desert.

Everything was run-down. There were paddocks, but all the fences were broken down, all the bores were broken down, all the horses were running bush. Those people had nothing. I gave myself three years to get everything set up for them.

I used to explain everything to the community – soon as you start your car it's costing money, you get money back from the cattle when we send them to the meatworks or market, that's how much we spend for fuel, that's how much we can spend on another tank or a bore – I'd be real open with them. We'd have a meeting, I'd have a bit of an idea what would be the best thing and I'd give them the reins to make their decision, because I had everything leading to the time they would become independent.

The previous manager, a whitefeller, had been there for six years and hardly had a visit from DAA [Department of Aboriginal Affairs], but as soon as I started the bureaucrats were backwards and forwards from Kununurra all the time, advising and interfering. Then the DEET got involved with it and the number of whitefellers heading out to Billiluna increased. They would not leave us alone.

I said to them, 'How come you're all coming out here now, when I'm trying to do something for these fellers and make things easier for them, make them a little bit independent of the government?'

'Ah, no,' they said, and another mob would come in. And another mob. I'm starting to get sick of this.

In the second year we sold a hell of a lot of cattle. I had contractors there by then, and we were fixing all the yards and the horse paddock, getting all the horses broken in and getting it back like a station should be.

Yet the government departments seemed to get all the people going against me. After I got all the cattle branded and they could see some progress, for some reason DAA started to tell the people, 'You don't need this bloke here,' arguing that they shouldn't be paying me wages. I think they could see the money we were making. I pointed out to them that you can have too many bosses. They were telling the Aboriginal people that they were the boss, and it was up to them to tell me what to do.

People started arguing about who was to be the boss. There were two groups and they started arguing. One mob wanted to form another community and a pastoral company to run cattle at Lake Gregory, or Malan. What had happened was the cattle were mostly around the lake, and that's where I built the yards and did all the development, and they reckoned I was favouring one group, sort of like a mob of overgrown kids. Before my time they had one chairperson. But when they started arguing, the two groups picked one chairperson from one side and one chairperson from the other side, and then they would argue about who was boss. The community was arguing that the pastoral company should be paying for electricity and water and the pastoral company was arguing that the community should be paying for their beef, and so it went on. Then some people started making trouble, getting drunk, making smart remarks in front of my wife; the mob from one community chasing the mob from the other community, looking for trouble because they were jealous.

Towards the end, when things were getting good, they all started getting cheeky, the opposite to what I reckoned they would be. I had been working with men since I was a kid, and most fellers, you give them respect and they give you respect, but this was different. I thought Aboriginal was Aboriginal – I never thought that they would start saying that, 'Ah, he's not from here, he's a Kija tribe, he's not a desert feller.' That really hurt me. I thought if you're black, you're black. I didn't wake up to these government departments and how they find ways of stopping progress.

One time we had to hurry up and get a shipment of cattle together. The station was running a bit low and I was half scared we wouldn't get the numbers that we had booked.

One old feller said to me, 'Don't worry, my boy, we won't starve. Gov'ment'll give us money.' We ended up getting the cattle numbers, but the attitude of that one bloke worried me. I go right back to blaming the government that created that attitude amongst Aborigines.

Towards the end DEET paid an advisor, a katiya feller, to come down from Darwin once every three months. He was supposed to be an expert with cattle and economic management. The Aboriginal people knew straight out he was the biggest jackeroo, yet it suited the group who were making the trouble to support him. They paid him $500 a day to come and have a meeting with them, just to turn up. He started trying to teach them the things I had already explained – where the money went and how much money they had, and so on – he used to explain the budget as having a billy can of money here and a billy can of money there, so the people used to call him Billycan. By the time he had finished they couldn't do anything. He went away in the end.

It's very hard for people to run something when they are used to being told what to do, and if they haven't got a good advisor who knows what he's doing, it's hopeless. Yet Aboriginal people are the best workers if they get respect and they're rewarded for their work. They're very good that way.

Finally I left them there and we came back to Halls Creek. I rang up Bedford Downs, where I knew the country, and asked for a job, to get some experience mustering in the chopper. The manager gave me the job, but when I got there he said that he couldn't afford to pay me wages, he'd have to put me off, and I had to ring up DEET to see if they could pay me. I knew that country better than any of the white people working there, but it was me that he wanted to put off. I just stood there. How could this happen to me? After all my life on that station I thought I'd be the last bloke they'd put off.

DEET ended up saying that they would pay me for a month, and the manager sent me mustering on Lansdowne. Another bloke went down to Lansdowne in the chopper and I drove the Toyota bull-catcher. I was looking forward to being in the chopper.

Somehow I passed the turn-off in the dark, but I could see tracks of shod horses on the road so I just kept following it. Next thing I ended up stalling this bloomin' Toyota bull-catcher in a rough creek, so I started walking. I thought I could hear an engine going and I knew they had a lighting plant in the stockcamp. I must have walked a good twenty k's or more that night. I kept lighting matches to see the horse tracks, and – bugger it! – I lost the track. So I had to sleep there by the roadside. I lit a fire and laid down on the ground.

Next morning it was a still day and I could see the smoke hanging on the river, so I knew the stockcamp wasn't too far away. As I was walking down towards the smoke I said to myself, Gee, I know this place. It was a rockhole where one old Aboriginal feller used to live when I was a kid. He wasn't even wearing clothes yet, he was still wearing his naga. All the other people that worked there, they knew him. They could speak the same language because we were all related.

I realised then it was nearly forty years since I had been there. That brought back some memories.

I remember that one night we had to swim the horses across this flooded creek to get to the yard just on the other side of the creek. We yarded all the cattle up, and the next morning when we got up we found that all the dogs were missing. What happened is that the gear must have worked loose on one of the pack mules and the packsaddle slipped off in the dark. When we went back looking for the dogs they were all there laying around the pack.

Anyway, I kept mustering with this other bloke in the chopper. One day I was flying with him and he said, 'Some bulls are baled up along the creek. I'll jump off here, you go and start pushing up the other mob.'

As I took off I spotted some cattle not far away, coming out of the scrub. Just as I started to bank to turn them, the red fuel-warning light came on. I just put her straight down in the spinifex and sang out to this bloke, 'Mate, you knew how many hours there were in this tank, you didn't tell me how many minutes I had left!' He had tried to set me up so that I would make a mess of the mustering, but I was saved by those cattle coming out of nowhere. I could have been killed. Lucky I was trained to keep an eye on the gauges. It's one of those things. I might have gone into the hills.

When we flew back to Bedford, he ended up pulling out and I took over the job. They had to muster the Springvale country again. I thought it was my dream come true, mustering on my home ground. I knew where all the waterholes were, I knew where the cattle would be camped and where they would walk to. I just had to poke along, land and wait for the cattle – I knew where they would be. But that dream was not to be.

The chopper needed cleaning so I decided to give it a good clean. I went right over it, cleaned underneath it, polished the glass, but when I got to the rotor I noticed a crack. I knew that chopper was well overdue for its overhaul and I just had a feeling it was not safe. The manager disagreed and I never did get to muster Springvale in a chopper. My life was worth more than that.

When we went back into Halls Creek a little block came up for sale, 2.2 hectares. I thought, What the hell. I could see a few grey hairs coming out now, and I decided that it was an opportunity to look after my family and build our own home. We borrowed the money and Evelyn and I got jobs in Halls Creek. Evelyn was working at Charlie Perkins' hostel and I got a job on the shire council, building roads, creek crossings, putting up signs – all that sort of thing.

•

One day, while Gilbert was working with the shire, Mick Coomb drove by in his old truck. 'It nearly broke my heart to see Gilbo working on the roads,' Mick recalled. 'Makes a man want to cry. I remember one time pickin' up a mob of cattle from

Springvale and Tom Quilty loaned me his mustering team, to give me a bit of a hand. They were so small their feet didn't reach the bottom of the saddle flap, but they could all do a man's work, every one of them. Gilbo has always been a top man, one of the best.'

Gilbert's response was characteristically curt. 'Old Mick said he felt like crying. I said to him, "How do you think I feel, Mick? But I haven't got time to cry. I've got a wife and kids to look after." '

The McAdams' house on the outskirts of Halls Creek is a corrugated iron structure festooned at the front with purple bougainvillea. It is set on a rise looking past two great glossy-leaved mango trees towards a low range of hills in the east. Gilbert's three horses graze the paddock. It is a house filled with people coming and going, although the family is growing up. Shane is playing VFL football in Sale after Geelong showed interest in his ability, and his wife Molly stays there with their one-year-old son Daimon from time to time. Gilbert and Evelyn have five daughters: Cherie and Debbie, with Debbie's son, come home from work in Kununurra on weekends; Kym and Carolyn are at school in Halls Creek; baby Jenice goes with her mother to the Ngoonjuwah Medical Service, where Evelyn is Director.

Gilbert looks towards the horizon, the low range of hills marking the boundary of Kija and Jaru country that became the original boundary of Moola Bulla. 'It's funny, even today I wonder what my other brother, the one who died, would have looked like. I look at Jenice and wonder if he would have looked like her as a baby. I think, Would he have looked like Shane, or Daimon? You seem to think more about these things as you get older.

'I think you've got to have that little dream that keeps you going. All I ever wanted was to live on Springvale, but I guess this is my Springvale now.'

# These Years

OF THE OLD people in Charlie's immediate family, his mother Burrel died in the 1980s and is buried at Halls Creek. Warragunye is buried in an unmarked sandy grave in the old native cemetery just out of Wyndham. The parameters of the cemetery are marked by steel star pickets and single wires. There are no signs to identify the place. Only Yunguntji lives to tell the story to his children, grandchildren and great-grandchildren.

Perhaps eight years after Charlie and the oher children were taken to Beagle Bay, in 1955, the West Australian government sold Moola Bulla to private interests and the Moola Bulla people were ejected overnight. They were given twenty-four hours' notice before they were removed in trucks, some to Halls Creek, others to Fitzroy Crossing, an isolated settlement on the edge of the Great Sandy Desert. There was no infrastructure in either Fitzroy Crossing or Halls Creek to cater for the influx. Missionaries of the United Aborigines Mission, with two days' notice, managed to feed the newcomers, who arrived well before the promised allocation of tents and provisions.

**Doris Fletcher:** I had four boys and one daughter on Moola Bulla. When the youngest was six months old, government kick us out. We didn't know what to do. We lost everything there – house, private things and all that. They never let us know. We didn't know the truck was coming in to get us and leave us there, way over there where the Nine Mile used to be, near Halls Creek. They left us there for a little while and then they took us to Fitzroy in the Christian place – church. We were camped there for a while. We were looking for job then. We were coming back little by little, getting job back here, out on the stations. Me and my husband went to Christmas Creek. He was doing saddling there. Then we went on to the place called Chestnut. My husband went to Gogo Station near Fitzroy, then we went back to Coopers Creek. Ord River Station, Flora Valley, Gordon Downs – we went to all those places. My husband, he work at Ord River Station, making saddles and those things, droving. And I come back here [to Halls Creek] and worked in the pub, to keep my kids at school.

My dad, he's buried in old station [Moola Bulla]. That man won't let us go back there. There's a lot of old people passed away and we left them, you know. Too many.

●

Moola Bulla was put up for auction in August 1993 and was passed in at $8.5 million. The asking price was quoted as $12 million. Pre-auction publicity described the property as 660 000 hectares of the best cattle country in the Kimberley, running 30 000 cattle and 400 horses. Despite their forced relocation, the Moola Bulla people maintain their traditional rights to the land. Moola Bulla is one of several areas in the Kimberley which may become the subject of native title claims.

Many of the children who travelled to Beagle Bay with Charlie on the back of the Chev truck did not return to their country.

Jackie Zohanna, the good student, won the lottery and lives in Broome. John Ross and Ernie Sara live and work in Derby. Ernie Sara went to La Grange from Beagle Bay and found out that his white father had actually been on Moola Bulla at the time he was there. 'Jack Knox his name was. He used to have a rodeo ground in Broome, and now I think his son is looking after the place. I didn't know he was my father until I was at La Grange and one of the old people told me. I said hullo and things, but we never ever knew each other much, and then he died, oh, a couple of years ago now. My mother died before that, in Derby here, and I didn't know until after.'

When Charlie left Moola Bulla in 1951 John Ross was eight years old. When John Ross was sixteen Bishop Raible gave him a holiday, and he never returned to Beagle Bay. Keith Kitchener, who was a baby on the back of the truck that took the children from Moola Bulla, stayed on at Beagle Bay. He never met his parents, but is philosophical about events, saying that if it had not been for the mission, the Aboriginal community at Beagle Bay would not be there now.

In the 1980s, control of all missions in the Kimberley, including Beagle Bay, passed to the respective Aboriginal communities and the Department of Aboriginal Affairs. The church and buildings remain. Some of the nuns have retired there. Father McGinley last visited the area in 1987 and was disappointed at what he found.

**Father McGinley:**   I was horrified to see the effects of commercialism and consumerism. Everybody has a TV and a video and they come back from Broome with horrible videos. And the kids are looking at rubbish. I said to the children,

'Why don't you have your song and your dances now?' 'Oh, that's old-fashioned.' And that's all. We can blame ourselves for that, because the whole white population of the area tried to make them into white people, and that's just terrible.

Many of the lads from Beagle Bay went to work as ringers on cattle stations in the Kimberley and the Northern Territory. Frank Byrne, like Charlie, made the decision to leave cattlework for better wages and stability once he married. He went to work-for a road construction company. A quietly spoken silver-haired man, he is now retired in Alice Springs. He spends a good bit of time on a little block out of town, where he runs a few calves, and mulling over the old days with Charlie.

**Charlie:**   That's just about the end of my story. After Valerie and I split up I worked with the Central Land Council as a field officer for about three years, and in 1990 I went out to Tanami Downs. In March '92 a horse fell on me, knocked me out and broke my knee and wrist. The Flying Doctor Service picked me up but I don't remember anything until I woke up in hospital in Alice Springs. I went back out to the station but the knee and wrist were still giving problems and I was referred to an orthopaedic surgeon in Adelaide. While I was in Adelaide I had a heart attack. I've only been able to do little jobs ever since.

I started thinking over all these years and everything that happened, and I thought I had to tell this story, for the kids and other people, so that they would know what happened in those days.

When I think about it now, I reckon a man's lucky if he gets to see the sun rise every morning and set at night, and if he can get three feeds a day.

I really believe that you come into this world with nothing and you should go back owing nobody. I hope I've got twenty years left in me yet, but in the end I reckon I'll go back cleanskin like I come.

---

# Acknowledgements

In the first place, acknowledgement must go to the people who contributed their stories to this book. It was a significant decision for members of Charlie's family and others to have part of their lives put into print. For most it was the first time they had spoken publicly of these things.

Mick Coomb, Father Roger McGinley and Cecil Rose also made important contributions.

Thanks are due to Monica Gregory and David Calwyn; the Aboriginal and Torres Strait Islander Arts Committee of the Australia Council for critical funding during the research stage; Simeon Becket and the Office of the Minister for Aboriginal Affairs; the Kimberley Language Resource Centre in Halls Creek; Rachel Bin Salleh and others at Magabala Books; the West Australian Department of Lands and Surveys; the Australian Stockmen's Hall of Fame; Chris Charles; Ushma Scales; Angus McClymont and Steve Baney.

Gary Foley and Sam Watson gave encouragement and advice during the writing of the manuscript. Bruce Sims showed confidence in the work from its conceptual stage and made succinct comment when it was most needed. Particular acknowledgement must go to Meredith Rose for her sensitive editing of the manuscript. My daughter Kirsty gave ongoing support.

This book would not have been written without the considerable input of my partner John Tregenza, who coordinated thousands of kilometres of travel and much of the oral research. His explanations of social structures, beliefs and meaning have been invaluable to someone whose understanding was largely limited to the theoretical disciplines of anthropology and history.

# A Note on the Writing of *Boundary Lines*

Unlike many books about Aboriginal people, this work was initiated by the Aboriginal participants themselves. In 1991 Charlie McAdam travelled from Alice Springs to Melbourne to enlist the help of my partner John Tregenza, whom he had known for some years, and myself.

Over the following two years, the three of us recorded some fifty hours of interviews, in Melbourne and on two trips to the Kimberley, which I then transcribed. During the editing process I maintained ongoing consultation with the story-tellers, to ensure that they approved of the written form of their statements and to clarify details that were unclear on tape. While individual stories have been reordered for the sake of continuity, the actual words of the storytellers remain unchanged.

The older contributors spoke Kija and Kriol, the latter being the common language of the Kimberley which evolved from the pidgin English taught to Aboriginal people by Europeans. Other contributors spoke Aboriginal English. Where it was necessary for me to translate, the structure, nuances and vocabulary have been retained but I have not used a spelling that would denote pronunciation of English words. Charlie's brief, which was reinforced by the Kija elders, was to record the story for future generations of Aboriginal and non-Aboriginal people in such a way that it would be accessible to a wide readership.

Elizabeth Tregenza
Melbourne, 1994

# Bibliography

## Books and Articles

Attwood, B., *The Making of the Aborigines*, Allen & Unwin, Sydney, 1989.

Battye, J.S., *Western Australia: A History from its Discovery to the Inauguration of the Commonwealth*, University of Western Australia Press, Perth, 1978.

Biskup, P., *Not Salves Not Citizens: The Aboriginal Problem in Western Australia 1889–1954*, University of Queensland Press, St Lucia, 1973.

Cameron, J.M.R., 'The Foundation of Western Australia Reconsidered' in *Studies in Western Australian History*, University of Western Australia Press, Perth, 1978.

Cole, T., *Hell West and Crooked*, Angus & Robertson, Sydney, 1988.

Coombs, H.C., McCann H., Ross H., and Williams, N.M. (eds), *Land of Promises: Aborigines and Development in the East Kimberley*, Centre for Resource and Environmental Studies, A.N.U., and Aboriginal Studies Press, Canberra, 1989.

Crawford, E. as told to Chris Walsh, *Over My Tracks*, Penguin, Melbourne, 1992.

Crawford, I.M., 'The Benedictine Mission at Kalumburu' in *Studies in Western Australian History*, University of Western Australia, November 1978.

Crough, G., *Visible and Invisible: Aboriginal People in the Economy of Northern Australia*, North Australian Research Unit and Nugget Coombs Forum for Indigeneous Studies, Darwin, 1993.

Dixon, R.A., and Dillon, M.C. (eds), *Aborigines and Diamond Mining: The Politics of Resource Development in the Eastern*

*Kimberley, Western Australia,* University of Western Australia Press, Perth, 1990.

Durack, M., *Keep Him My Country,* Constable, London, 1955.

——*Kings in Grass Castles,* Constable, London, 1959.

——*The Rock and the Sand,* Constable, London, 1969.

Elkin, A.P., *The Australian Aborigines: How to understand them,* Angus & Robertson, Sydney, 1964.

Edwards, H., *Kimberley: Dreaming to Diamonds,* Hugh Edwards, Perth, 1991.

Faine, J., *Lawyers in the Alice: Aboriginals and Whitefella's Law,* Federation Press, Sydney, 1993.

Franklin, M.A., *Black and White Australians: An Inter-racial history 1788–1975,* William Heinemann, Melbourne, 1976.

Green, N., *The Oombulgurri Story: A Pictorial History of the People of Oombulgurri 1884–1988,* Focus Education Services, Cottesloe, 1988.

Harris, B., *The Proud Champions: Australia's Aboriginal Sporting Heroes,* Little Hills Press, Sydney, 1989.

Hasluck, P., *Black Australians: A Survey of Native Policy in Western Australia 1829–1897,* Melbourne University Press, Melbourne, 1942.

Hawke, S.J., 'The North West Massacres', *Sydney Morning Herald,* 1 June 1988, p 8.

Horton, D. (ed), *The Encyclopaedia of Aboriginal Australia,* Australian Institute of Aboriginal and Torres Strait Islander Studies, Canberra, 1994.

Huegel, Fr. Francis, and Nailon, Sr. Brigida, *This is Your Place: Beagle Bay Mission 1890–1990,* Beagle Bay Community and Magabala Books, Broome, 1990.

Hunter, E., *Aboriginal Health and History: Power and Prejudice in Remote Australia,* Cambridge University Press, Oakleigh, 1993.

Kimberley Language Resource Centre, *Kija Wordbook,* Jawa Curriculum Support, Broome, 1990.

——*Moola Bulla: In the Shadow of the Mountain*, Magabala Books, Broome, 1995.

Langford, R., *Don't Take Your Love to Town*, Penguin, Melbourne, 1988.

Lyon, P., and Parsons, M., *We Are Staying: The Alyawarre Struggle for Land at Lake Nash*, IAD Press, Alice Springs, 1989.

McGrath, A., *Born in the Cattle*, Allen & Unwin, Sydney, 1987.

McGregor, A., and Chester, Q., *The Kimberley: Horizons of Stone*, Hodder & Stoughton, Melbourne, 1992.

McKnight, T.L., *The Long Paddock: Australia's Travelling Stock Routes*, University of New England, Armidale, 1977.

McLeod, D., *How the West was Lost: The Native Question in the Development of Western Australia*, D. McLeod, Port Hedland, 1984.

Marshall, P. (ed.), *Raparapa: All Right, Now We Go 'Longside the River: Stories from the Fitzroy River Drovers*, Magabala Books, Broome, 1988.

Quilty, T., *The Drover's Cook and Other Verses*, Hesperian Press, Carlisle, 1958.

Rosser, B., *Dreamtime Nightmares*, Penguin, Melbourne, 1985.

Reynolds, H. (ed), *Aborigines and Settlers: The Australian Experience 1788–1939*, Cassell, Sydney, 1972.

——*The Other Side of the Frontier: Aboriginal Resistance to the European Invasion of Australia*, Penguin, Melbourne, 1990.

——*Dispossession: Black Australians and White Invaders*, Allen & Unwin, Sydney, 1989.

——*With the White People: The Crucial Role of Aborigines in the Exploration and Development of Australia*, Penguin, Melbourne, 1990.

Rintoul, S., *The Wailing: A National Black Oral History*, William Heinemann, Melbourne, 1993.

Rowley, C.D., *The Remote Aborigines*, ANU Press, Canberra, 1971.

———'Outcasts in White Australia', *Aboriginal Policy and Practice*, Vol II, ANU Press, Canberra, 1971.

Sawrey, Durack, et al, *The Stockman: Australian Outback Heritage*, Lansdowne, Sydney, 1984.

Somerville, et al, *The Sun Dancin': People and Place in Coonabarabran*, Aboriginal Studies Press, Canberra, 1994.

Stanner, W.E.H., *After the Dreaming: Black and White Australians – An Anthropologist's View*, Australian Broadcasting Commission, Sydney, 1969.

Thomas, R., with Akerman, K., Macha, M., Christensen, W., and Caruana, W., *Roads Cross: The Paintings of Rover Thomas*, National Gallery of Australia, Canberra, 1994.

Wanganeen, E., *Justice Without Prejudice: The Development of the Aboriginal Legal Rights Movement in South Australia*, South Australian College of Advanced Education Aboriginal Studies and Teacher Education Centre, Adelaide, 1986.

### Acts of Parliament (Western Australia)

No. 14 of 1905: an Act to make provision for the better protection and care of the Aboriginal inhabitants of Western Australia and its amendment in 1911.

No. 43 of 1936: an Act to amend the Aborogines Act, 1905.

No. 23 of 1944: an Act to provide for the full acquisition of full rights of citizenship by aborigine natives.

No. 64 of 1954: an Act to amend the Native Administration Act, 1905–1947.

No. 79 of 1963: an Act to consolidate and amend the law relating to and providing for the Welfare of the Native Inhabitants of Western Australia; and for incidental and other purposes.

### Maps

Visual information was derived from an exhibition of the artists of Turkey Creek at Tandanya in Adelaide in 1993, and from Power of the

Land: Masterpieces of Aboriginal Art, National Gallery of Victoria, 1994. Several maps were important:

Map drawn by Yunguntji on the ground at Bedford Downs, 1993.

Maps drawn by Tjulaman at Caroline Pool, 1993, and Banjo Bore, 1994.

Map drawn by Charlie McAdam at Banjo Bore, 1994.

Map of stock routes at Jones Store, Newcastle Waters.

*Aboriginal Land and Population*, Natmap, Canberra, 1980.

*Northern Terrritory Pastoral and General Tenure Map*, Northern Territory Departments of Lands, Housing and Local Government, Darwin, 1994

*East Kimberley,* Department of Land Administration, Perth, 1989.

### SOUTHERN SKY, WESTERN OVAL   Martin Flanagan

Martin Flanagan spent 1993 with AFL football team, Footscray. In 1989, the Footscray Football Club had almost ceased to exist. Three years later, under coach Terry Wheeler, the Bulldogs had gone within one game of playing in the AFL grand final. Flanagan was given access to coaching staff, executives and supporters. He was with the players before and after matches. The result is a book about Australian football written from within. It's a book which asks questions. Can players withstand the physical stress of the modern game? Can the smaller clubs survive? And, most importantly, does the Australian game have a future?

*Southern Sky, Western Oval* traces the story of one season in the 110-year-old history of a proud working-class club, which, in itself, reflects Australian history.

'Martin Flanagan must never be allowed to stop writing about football . . . I say this because he is the only football writer I have read who is so good I think he could nearly describe a heartbeat . . .'

Don Watson

## ALSO FROM McPHEE GRIBBLE

**GATTON MAN**   Merv Lilley

Below the Darling Downs in the Queensland district of Gatton on Boxing Day 1898, the raped and bashed bodies of the Murphys, two sisters and a brother, were found in a paddock alongside their dead horse, beginning one of the longest murder investigations in Australian history.

Short of a century later, Merv Lilley recounts life on the land in the Queensland he knew between the wars, life under the terrifying and perverted rule of his father. On the way he dismantles the myths of the little Aussie battler, Dad and Dave, the man on the land, and reconstructs instead a violent and male-dominated reign of terror, the brutalisation of the bush. He also follows the cold trail of the Gatton killer through transcript and folk tale, circumstance and sensation, to his own doorstep.

'Art and murder combined in one family saga.'

Stephen Knight